PEASANT MOBILIZATION AND SOLIDARITY

STUDIES OF DEVELOPING COUNTRIES (formerly *Non European Societie⸱*)

edited by

prof. dr. L. H. Janssen S.J. (Tilburg), prof. dr. A. J. F. Köbben (Amsterdam), prof. dr. R. A. J. van Lier Wageningen), prof. dr. G. W. Locher (Leiden) and prof. dr. J. D. Speckmann (Leiden).

B. F. GALJART

Peasant mobilization and solidarity

1976
VAN GORCUM, ASSEN/AMSTERDAM

ISBN 90 232 1381 5

This publication was sponsored by:
Netherlands Organization for the Advancement of Pure Research (ZWO)
The Hague, the Netherlands

Printed in the Netherlands

Table of contents

Preface to the Dutch edition

The field research in Chile upon which the greater part of this book is based, was carried out between June 1969 and September 1970. From the Netherlands Organization for the Advancement of Pure Research (ZWO) I received a scholarship which covered my research and travelling expenses, while the Agricultural University of Wageningen granted me leave to spend over a year in Chile. I am exceedingly grateful to both organizations for the opportunity thus offered me, but accept sole responsibility for the manner in which I availed of it.

In Chile I received hospitality from the Instituto de Capacitación e Investigación en Reforma Agraria, established in Santiago. This organization was of particular help in providing me with introductions. I am grateful to Solon Baraclough and David Alaluf for their readiness to smooth my path with a note or a telephone call. In addition I had frequent contact with a number of members of the scientific staff. I am particularly grateful to Hugo Zemelman, Sergio Gomez and Emilio Klein for their many services, large and small. There is no room to mention here all the CORA and INDAP officials who gave up their time so freely to an interchange of ideas, introduced me to farming communities and allowed me to accompany them on their field trips. An exception must be made for Julio Manriquez and Alejandro Ruiz Lamas, who became my friends.

Since my research entailed visits to a large number of places, I got to know many peasants and peasant leaders. Although the exact nature of my intentions may not always have been clear to them, I was treated everywhere with great courtesy and helpfulness. My intentions have now become fact in the form of a book. I hope that by correctly interpreting their thoughts, actions and aspirations I have redeemed at least part of the debt I owe them.

The research was carried out during the last years of President Frei's government and the book written during the three years that President Allende was in power. After it was finished the army seized power in Chile. Since the book is not intended as a description of Chilean affairs but rather as an attempt at sociological theorizing on peasants who organize and on the vicissitudes of their organizations, I do not believe that the altered situation in Chile since 1970 has affected its validity. It does sadden me though that it should appear at a time when those to whom it was addressed, albeit obliquely, whose idealism I frequently countered with my more pragmatic approach, have lost their jobs or been obliged to leave Chile. The fact that I do not always share their opinions does not mean that I reject their aspirations. On the contrary, this book is intended as a contribution towards achieving those objectives. Our discussion was rudely interrupted by outsiders, but will surely be continued at another time and in another place.

Wageningen, September 1973

1

Preface to the English edition

Thanks to a further grant from ZWO, the Dutch text, after some minor revisions, has been translated into English. I am grateful to Rudi van Lier, Emanuel de Kadt and Dick Papousek for their critical reading of the Dutch edition of the book. Some of the blemishes they pointed out have been eliminated. Others I have left in, for the reader's sake, or for my own. I owe gratitude to Mrs Mary Foran for the care with which she translated the book, and to Ineke Smeets for the construction of an index.

Leiden, June 1975

2

Chapter 1   Problem and theoretical framework

This book deals with the sociological aspects of the mobilization of and solidarity among peasants. Although most of the data were gathered in Chile, I believe that my conclusions possess a wider validity. Unlike other authors, who reserve the term peasants for independent small agrarian producers, I understand by this term all those more or less poor people who earn their living in agriculture. This would include those who work on the land solely for payment in money[1]. I shall call these people peasants and, whenever it becomes necessary to distinguish between categories, speak of smallholders (that is, independent producers, whether they own the land they work, rent it, or sharecrop it) and agricultural labourers (either permanent or temporary).

Some people might regard a sociological study of the political mobilization of peasants, of their co-operation and solidarity, as a fairly unimportant and specialized exploration of one fraction of the stupendous development problem which confronts the countries of the Third World. Such an impression, however, would be incorrect. For a time it was thought that development would have to consist chiefly of rapid industrialization. Now, however, the view is growing that the solution to the immense problems of poverty, unemployment, low agricultural production, low rates of internal savings, in short, of underdevelopment, must be sought in the first instance in the rural areas, in the agricultural sector. It may be said of the majority of developing countries that in the course of the next twenty years, their future will be decided in the countryside and by these peasants. It will prove of crucial importance to determine what they want and what they do not, what is capable of arousing their enthusiasm and what is not, with whom they associate and are willing to co-operate and with whom they are not.

The mobilization and solidarity which are the subject of this book occur within a particular structural and cultural context, namely that of an underdeveloped country in Latin America. I do not intend here to deal exhaustively with the problem of underdevelopment. It will, however, be necessary to touch upon it insofar as the thinking on this problem has influenced the central theme of this study and its theoretical framework. This is all the more essential since my theoretical framework differs from that of many other rural sociological and anthropological studies with regard to agricultural development. Until recently these studies concentrated mainly on the peasants' resistance to change, their conservatism, their apathy, in short upon the obstacles to development arising from their culture[2].

Traditional was understood as synonymous with being opposed to change. Elsewhere (Galjart, 1971a) I have postulated that such a focus must inevitably lead to an emphasis on the transfer of knowledge and the elimination of cultural opposition, and a neglect of those obstacles to change which are rooted in the social and economic structure. The focus itself results from the uncritical export to the underdeveloped countries of both the

3

concepts (tradition and modernity) and the approach (research on the level of the single village community) which had characterized sociological research into agricultural development in the industrial countries. This focus was understandable in those countries where the provision of credit and price policies had minimized the braking effect of a lack of capital upon agricultural development (and in so doing increased the importance of other brakes, such as the cultural). In addition, expansion in other sectors of the economy had cushioned and obscured the results of agricultural development, the disappearance from farming first of the farmers' sons and the paid agricultural workers and later of the farm owners who had no one to succeed them. These farmers vanished from the farming scene. However, this frame of reference cannot be applied in the underdeveloped countries since it leads to the neglect of what is precisely the most important factor in agricultural development, namely the agrarian structure.

One important characteristic of an underdeveloped country is that the problem of development is regarded as central by the government, the political parties and large sectors of the population. This is indeed the automatic result of the general desire for a higher standard of living. It also means that the political struggle in these countries is largely dominated by the various views of and attitudes toward the problem of development.

In the course of the past fifteen years, thinking on this problem has changed in Latin America. Explanations of underdevelopment in terms of values and attitudes which people hold have come under attack for being too partial if not erroneous.

Also, it has become evident that industrialization, aimed at the domestic market and intended as a substitute for imports, could not prevent economic stagnation. Although it is impossible yet to speak of a consensus, certain schematic trends of thought have emerged, all implying similar essential changes in social structure.

One trend sees the problem of underdevelopment as a consequence of dependence on and exploitation by the developed capitalist countries. Since this state of affairs is perpetrated by the ruling classes, which benefit from it, radical structural changes cannot be but the outcome of a socialist revolution. The entire productive organization of society, including that of agriculture, should become socialist if the country is to put itself on the road to development.

A second school of thought prefers to explain the development problem in Latin America as arising from the economic structure which has grown up through the years within these countries. During the crisis of the thirties most countries began a programme of industrialization to replace imports of non-durable consumer goods. The constant lack of foreign currency later led to further industrialization to save on imports of durable consumer goods. The market for these was very small in view of the very unequal income distribution. Although this process could make more progress in the larger countries than in the small, it everywhere led to a worsening of the terms of exchange for agrarian products: industry had to make its profit from high prices, and not from a large turnover, which simply wasn't there. Yet the agrarian stagnation which results from the unfavourable terms of exchange and the unchanged income distribution cannot but hamper industrial growth. Evers & Vossenaar (1971) show that in Latin America, unlike other developing countries, the influence of population growth on industrial expansion exceeds that of a growth in income. This is due to the highly unequal income distribution. They

4

therefore conclude that further expansion will only be possible via structural changes: an end to stagnation in agriculture and the redistribution of incomes throughout society. Why the seemingly apathetic acceptance by agriculture of this relatively worsening position? It seems to me that the reasons are twofold. Insofar as smallholders still practise subsistence farming, they escape this process in part[3]. In addition the large landowner is often able to make his tenants, share-croppers or workers absorb part at least of the consequences of agriculture's unfavourable position.

Whereas these two trends of thought are not very explicit about the precise productive organization that is to result from agrarian reform, in Chile in the sixties ideas with regard to this problem were developed by catholic groupings who wished above all to end the socially marginal position of the peasant population and create a society consistent with human dignity. They rejected the absolute power of the state, so evident in the European socialist countries (cf. Silva & Chonchol, 1969) and preferred instead communal enterprises, the fusion of labour and capital in the same persons. We see thus that, starting from different positions, various observers came to regard the social structure and notably the mode of ownership of the means of production in the countryside as a problem.

The tasks assigned to a reformed agriculture are both economic (the creation of an internal market, an increase in production so as to cut down on the import of food and create more job opportunities) and social, particularly in Chile (equality and incorporation in the national polity). Land reforms carried out in Bolivia and Mexico had shown that the division of the land into family farms as desired by the peasants, had diminished their poverty and marginality only slightly and had left many peasants out in the cold.

This brief outline shows that the problem of peasant mobilization and solidarity cannot be viewed exclusively in terms of the desires, aims and insights of the peasants themselves. It must also be viewed within the larger framework of the national development effort and the political struggle for consensus regarding this effort. This is not only because what the peasants want and do will influence these efforts, but also because the political leaders and movements in their turn will seek to influence the peasants' aspirations and actions. The last two chapters of this book will examine in some detail the extent to which these two 'intentions' converged or diverged in Chile. Now, however, we shall deal with those theories on individual and local group level which served as guide-lines to my study.

It has been an implicit assumption of this study and one of which I only became really aware as I collated my data, that peasants view their interests primarily in local terms, that is to say in terms of the social structure and the distribution of resources as they are found in their local community. I am now convinced that this assumption is correct and hope that my results will convince the reader as well.

A hypothesis developed by Röling (1970) concerning the reasons motivating individual peasants to change, provides a suitable starting point for elaborating a theory based on this assumption. Röling defines development as the increasing possibility of the individual to control his own environment. He postulates that a peasant, noting a difference between the situation he experiences and the situation which he covets, (not as a gratuitous, wishful dream, but measured against the situation which he sees others enjoying), will first of all wish to eliminate this difference by altering his own experienced situation in such a way as to bring about the one desired. He will then try to discover how this may be done, and will do his best to put into practice the knowledge gained. This voluntaristic model does not, of course, describe what actually happens. Only too often the peasants are incapable of following a planned course of action. Röling does not preoccupy himself overmuch with why this is so, but postulates that a permanent difference between conditions experienced and desired gives rise to frustration which the peasants attempt either to suppress or to overcome by various reactions. We shall return to these reactions which are thought to give rise to particular cultural patterns. The fact to be stressed here is that Röling's theory makes it possible to seek the obstacles to innovation and agrarian development primarily in circumstances outside the individual peasant, notably in the social structure and in the distribution of land. Moreover, a theory which attributes cultural resistance to development not to tradition but to frustration arising from previous attempts to achieve development, chimes much better with the fact that new opportunities in traditional peasant cultures are often rapidly seized upon and exploited. In an earlier study of Brazil (Galjart, 1968) I found no indication that the peasants resisted the introduction of new techniques or crops. The entire theory of the traditional stick-in-the-mud peasants in non-western countries is, if not inaccurate, at least based upon assumptions which are usually too simplistic for the circumstances.

What is the actual situation of a peasant in Latin America on the local community level? In answering this question I shall introduce a second assumption which seems to me correct but for which we have as yet no proof. This is that the peasant's chance of survival and development possibilities are determined by the (local) distribution of what is for him the most important resource, namely land. In a later model, to be dealt with in detail in Chapter 3 (see p. 22) the assumption is made that once this resource is closed, the rivalry for land between households – or other groups – can result in three types of division, or, to use Röling's terms, three different experienced situations. These are:
a. The distribution of land among the households displays a fairly high measure of equality.
b. The distribution of land among the households is unequal, but the great majority has access to land.
c. The land is in the hands of one or a few individuals. The remaining households have no land of their own, or hardly any although they may have the use of land belonging to the monopolist.

In situation (a), all the households dispose of a roughly equal quantity of land. Examples of situation (a) may be found in the settlements of European colonists in Southern Brazil, in most of the modern colonization and irrigation projects and in some farming communities, whether they be Indian or not. The Indian communities included in this category are those to which no one can lay any claim of domain and which have not been deprived of land to any extent. Examples of situation (b) are the communities of independent peasants to be found in all Latin American countries. Here economic differentiation can admittedly be found but not to the extent that the land may be said to belong to only a handful of individuals.

Examples of situation (c) are the communities or local groups which either rent or sharecrop, or work for wages on land belonging to one or a couple of owners; the population of haciendas or plantations. I also include under (c) those communities of peasants – usually Indian – who, while possessing a certain amount of land, which they work themselves, have, in the course of the centuries, lost the larger part of their land tò the surrounding haciendas which enclose the territory belonging to the community. İn category (c) thus we find not only independent producers (minifundia) but tenant farmers, sharecroppers and wage workers. In some cases the group displays a considerable amount of cohesion, but according as they have less access to land, either as owners or tenants, it tends to fragment.

My research in Chile dealt with peasants in situation (b) and groups of agricultural labourers on large enterprises who found themselves in category (c).

It is clear that peasants, depending upon the situation in which they find themselves and upon the specific manner in which they are involved in the process of production, may have both similar and varying interests. Their interests are similar in that they are poor in a society, and often in a local community in which wealth, income, and to a certain extent power, are concentrated in the hands of a fairly restricted élite. In such circumstances how can the peasant gain more control over his surroundings?

1. As an individual he can try, by his own efforts, to join the élite, that is to say acquire the attributes of the élite. In practice this implies migration, an attempt to improve his education and to exploit the possibilities in agricultural enterprise, insofar as these exist. As we have observed a great deal of earlier rural sociological research has concerned itself chiefly with this possibility of development.
2. He can, as an individual, attempt to improve his situation by means of patronage. Patronage is, in principle, a dyadic relationship between people of unequal social standing, whereby the party possessing the higher status dispenses economic advantages to the party of the lower. In exchange the advantaged party rewards his patron with prestige, political support and other services[4].
3. He can, by co-operating with his social equals, attempt to improve his lot and theirs at the same time. So long as this attempt does not prove a flash in the pan, it will usually find expression in some organization which promotes the peasants' interests.

In my Brazilian research (Galjart, 1968) I found, among peasants in situation (b), attempts at 1 and 2 but only abortive attempts at 3. I even came to the conclusion that the active solicitation for patronage explained why solidarity between social equals was so weak in Brazil.

It is my opinion, however, that only co-operation can help relieve the poverty of smallholders and agricultural labourers. For the latter (situation (c)) this seems self-evident: it is their association in a trade union which provides them with the necessary 'countervailing power' to insist on higher wages and better living conditions. Their interests and those of their employers i.e. the landed proprietors, are to a large extent in conflict[5]. Regarding the smallholders in situations (a) and (b) the position is different in that they have no direct local opponents with the exception, perhaps, of merchants. They are menaced by a complex of phenomena, such as unfavourable terms of exchange, the increase in socio-economic inequality which accompanies the development of farming units into family businesses, and employment opportunities in other sectors of the economy which are insufficient to absorb the expected exodus from agriculture. For that matter the limited capacity of industry and the service sector to absorb any surplus labour affects all categories of the agrarian population. Publications issued by FAO (1969) and ILO (1971) predict that in many developing countries agriculture will have to provide work for not less but more people in the coming decades. Agricultural development after the West European model based on family units and with the less successful, superfluous smallholders and agricultural labourers drifting from the land would condemn the majority of Latin American peasants to permanent and even increasing poverty. This can only be prevented by their working together and so achieving advantages of scale to which they could not aspire as individuals. In this way they could also assert their 'countervailing power' on the markets and thus nibble away to some extent at the large trade margins. In all probability too a greater equality of income will have to be created by the collectivization of some or all of the means of production. In West European countries such as the Netherlands, the shrinkage of job opportunities in agriculture and the growth of socio-economic inequality among farmers has not been arrested by an extensive network of service co-operatives (Weerdenburg, 1970, p. 6 f.)[6].

The question of what sociological factors influence co-operation among peasants may be divided up into a number of subsidiary points.

Firstly, what sociological factors influence the mobilization process which leads peasants to set up associations for their mutual advantage and to enter into other new co-operative links? In Chapter 3 we shall develop a theory regarding those factors which, on the level of society and local community influence the mobilization of agricultural labourers into syndicates. In Chapter 4 this theory is tested to some extent against quantitative data relating to Chilean communities, while Chapter 5 develops a theory with regard to the mobilization into co-operatives of peasants who find themselves in situations (a) and (b).

A second question concerns the individual differences between those who are mobilized and those who are not (or, to put it another way, members and non-members). In Chapter 6 hypotheses are developed and tested regarding the differences between members and non-members of syndicates on the one hand and of co-operatives on the other.

The data are derived chiefly from a survey. In Chapter 8 (leaving Chapter 7 aside for the moment) we inquire into those factors which influence solidarity among peasants in their new associations. We have already suggested that co-operation, even though born of the participants' expectation of individual economic advantage, cannot succeed without a certain readiness to sacrifice on the peasants' part. Solidarity as an attitude becomes increasingly important according as more sacrifices are required of the peasants than mere participation in associations. Since this was the case in Chile and since – should I prove correct in my prediction that in the future a certain degree of social and economic equality will be created among peasants in other developing countries through the collectivization of the means of production – government agricultural policy in other countries will perhaps come to be determined by what rural sociologists understand by solidarity, it seems to me important to dissect this concept theoretically with the aid of data gathered during my research. In countries where the government attaches importance to a certain social equality, it is often the sociologists who are asked what measures the peasants will accept to achieve this equality and what measures they will not. In such a situation solidarity is a key concept and sociologists who have not kept abreast of their subject are inclined to proffer rash recommendations which not only fail to advance equality but may well result in the peasant having to endure a lower than necessary standard of living.

Our research was carried out within a very well defined context: the Chilean central valley between August 1969 and August 1970. This context influenced the research and even the approach to the problem. In 1965 the Frei government had embarked on a programme of land reform which included the organization of the small farmers and agricultural labourers. This reform consisted in the acquisition, under various pretexts, of enterprises larger than 80 hectares of irrigated land or that amount of land which might be considered the local equivalent. After the expropriation, these enterprises were run by the workers living (and working) on them at the time under the supervision of the government body CORA (Corporación de Reforma Agraria) which was responsible for carrying out the land reform. For the first three years, as laid down by the land reform law, the enterprise, now called asentamiento, would be organized along communal lines. After this the peasants would be allowed to choose whether they wished to retain this communal enterprise or break it up into family units which, though united in a co-operative, would be otherwise independent. They could also opt for a mixed form, a communal farm in which houses and gardens would be private property. In any case the peasants themselves would exercise control, without the intervention of CORA.

For the agricultural workers INDAP (Instituto de Desarrollo Agropecuario), another government body, founded syndicates, as for that matter did other groups, whether catholic or socialist—communist orientated. The syndicates were regarded as militant organizations to promote the workers' interests. They would also serve as a preparation or training school for the self government which would come with the expropriation of the large estates. Syndicates were established in a community and had to number at least a hundred members; sub-sections, known as committees, could be started up in a particular enterprise as soon as there were six members. Where one farm was unable to provide six members, one committee was allowed to take in several enterprises. After some time the syndicates united on the provincial level in a federation. A number of federations could, in their turn, proceed to the setting up of a national confederation.

Finally, at the outset, the independent smallholders were encouraged by INDAP to unite in local committees at neighbourhood level. These were intended chiefly to serve as channels for the various forms of credit provided by INDAP. When, after two years, the committees proved too small to develop into viable co-operatives, the setting up of municipal co-operatives was encouraged, each comprising a number of the original committees. The committee remained in existence as a local but no longer independent subdivision whose members met regularly. Representatives of the various committees had to maintain contact with the executive of the co-operative. Since in many localities INDAP started to provide credit only via the co-operative, the peasants were to some extent obliged to join. In many localities too, but again by no means everywhere, INDAP advanced capital credit only to communal groups which had developed through co-option and which had decided to co-operate in production – usually chickens or pigs.

We see therefore that on the asentamientos at least and in the farming co-operatives, not alone was affiliation required but acceptance of and participation in communal production as well. Government policy displayed a certain preference for this form of production, certainly insofar as the smallholders and asentados were concerned. The political parties to the left of the Christian-Democrats showed the same preference. In these circumstances solidarity implied the acceptance of the communal form of production and, naturally, of those values which government policy desired the peasants to practice: social equality, participation in community affairs and national policy, and economic development[7].

In Chapter 7 we shall discuss which factors influence participation, dealing principally with the differences between leaders and members of associations.

I conclude this chapter with a warning. Strictly speaking the results of this study are valid only for those groups of Chilean peasants whom I researched. However, as is already apparent from the title of this book, I believe myself that the results in general will prove to have a much wider validity. This fact notwithstanding, the reader would be well advised to refrain from attempting to apply these results indiscriminately to all small farmers in Latin America. This study confirms a number of hypotheses formulated for Chile, but for the rest of Latin America hypotheses they must remain.

Notes

1 In a study which deals with the role played by peasants in Chilean society, it will not do to exclude in advance a section of the agrarian working population, the agricultural labourers. This is all the more true since their number is so large. Yet there are also theoretical reasons for including the agricultural labourers among the peasants. The first is that a person can run a small farm of his own and at the same time work for somebody else. The second is that it seems to me nonsensical to regard an agricultural labourer as a non-peasant, while then proceeding to classify him among the peasants as part owner of an expropriated hacienda.

2 Even in a recent book like that of Rogers (1969) the most important obstacles to social change are still localized in the 'subculture of peasantry'.

3 Scott (1972) shows for central Chile that more than 75% of his respondents (smallholders) use more than half of their total production to supply their own needs.

4 The literature on patronage is very extensive. See for instance, Boissevain (1966) and Mühlmann & Llaryora (1968) on patronage in Europe; Foster (1963) and Hutchinson (1966) on this phenomenon in Latin American countries.

5 I shall refrain for the moment from going into other possible consequences of a wage conflict, such as a decreasing demand for labour in agriculture due to accelerated mechanization, a changeover to less labour intensive crops, etc.

6 It may perhaps be useful to point out that the view that agricultural labourers and peasant farmers need to co-operate is not necessarily theirs, but mine. This is particularly true of the assertion that peasants must also achieve a certain co-operation in production if growing socio-economic differentiation among them and the trickling away of the poorest and least successful towards the towns, is to be prevented. In many countries the enforcement of co-operation in production has led in the beginning to a lower aggregate production (which is more justly divided). Ultimately the opinion that a certain social equality must be created in agriculture is based not only on the conviction that this is possible without a noticeable decrease in the total production, but also upon a value.

I shall adhere to this value but also believe that a too radical leveling out, notably the elimination of a direct link between reward and achievement, is harmful to production and is therefore undesirable.

7 Some may doubt whether the authorities were really in earnest about the realization of these values. Government policy certainly varied according to time and place, and it is also certain that the most fervent supporters of the realization of the above-mentioned values came to doubt the seriousness of the government's intentions after a couple of years. As a result of this many left the government and the party (the first to go being Jacques Chonchol, then vice-president of INDAP).

10

It is also certain that within both the christian-democratic party and the government, influence was brought to bear by people who certainly did not desire socialization, while the claims of sectors other than the peasants upon scanty government funds led to a shortage in the funds necessary for the reform of the agrarian structure (cf. Chonchol, 1970).

Chapter 2 Research methods and the researcher's values

2.1 The preliminary investigation

So that the reader may judge for himself what value to put on my data and conclusions it is useful to examine in some depth the way in which the research was carried out. Various phases were involved and my approach to each depended upon how I viewed the problem. The problem has, for a very long time, been: what are we to understand by solidarity. The problem originated in Brazil where I stayed from the middle of 1962 to the middle of 1965. Plans for researching solidarity were already being considered then, and I even got so far as to hold a series of discussions on that theme with my colleague and friend, Carlos Alberto de Medina. I also began to peruse the literature on the subject and have continued with this study by fits and starts on my return to the Netherlands, despite the claims of other work. At that time I saw solidarity as the attitude of which co-operation was the perceptible result. This may have been because I had concluded in Itaguaí (Galjart, 1968) that the colonists did not co-operate because they had no sense of solidarity. The books I read did not focus upon any specific problem but consisted of practically everything I could lay my hands upon, there on the spot, which dealt with aspects of co-operation and with cohesion. Although I drew up a plan of research in the summer of 1968 and sent it in in order to be able to apply for research funds, I still felt confused. This confusion sprang in large measure from the inclination to view solidarity as a quality which a person either showed in all relationships or in none. Only very gradually I came to understand that the concept could be applied only in relation to a definite group. The plan of research was particularly concerned with tracking down the differences – in structural and personality traits – between peasants who collaborated with others and those who did not. Shortly before my departure for Chile someone observed, quite correctly, that co-operation need not necessarily be based on solidarity, but could also for example spring from self-interest.

When, therefore, I arrived in Chile in June 1969, I had as it were two problems: solidarity and co-operation. The latter, no matter how motivated, was perhaps the more important for the development of the rural areas. Particularly important was co-operation in the modern peasant organizations, the syndicates and co-operatives, in other words the affiliation and degree of participation in those associations. The choice of concerning myself particularly with those newly founded organizations seemed an obvious one but it strongly influenced my method of work. There seemed little sense in staying for any length of time in a small preasant community; one could shadow a peasant for weeks on end without noticing once that he was a member of an organization. Another argument against research in only a small number of local communities, say two or three, was the fact that both the syndicates and the co-operatives were organized on municipality level, a unit which comprised several local communities, sometimes more than twenty.

Every large agricultural enterprise and every concentration of peasants constituted such a local community. I doubted whether it was worthwhile to devote much time to a thorough study of three such units, apart altogether from the fact that it would be difficult to obtain permission from the owner of a large estate to come in and do a prolonged study of a phenomenon which could, in itself, hardly be expected to appeal to him. And, strictly speaking, on the local community level I would not even be able to obtain an overall view of the entire co-operative or syndicate. For these reasons I decided to visit a much greater number of places for a shorter time and, besides interviewing leaders and members of the organizations, to be particularly assiduous in attending meetings. These meetings were the occasions above all others when co-operation might become visible in the behaviour of the peasants and when, I hoped, in dealing with the agenda, any difficulties they had might be revealed. This attending meetings as an observer at every level of the organizations turned out very well for me. My presence was apparently not resented: people were not inhibited by the outsider. In addition this method did indeed provide me with considerable data which would have been much more difficult to acquire by questioning. Now it was possible to ask concrete questions at the end of the meeting, if there was anything I didn't understand. Naturally I was unable to ferret out the local background of every incident or case, but to compensate for this I gained a good impression of the extent to which certain problems, attitudes and incidents occurred generally. As Glaser and Strauss have written (1967), the researcher's insight into a particular, recurrent phenomenon, grows to the point of surfeit where he believes that henceforth he can safely take it for granted. In this way I have visited and attended meetings of organizations in the municipalities of La Serena (province of Coquimbo), Puente Alto, Melipilla, San Antonio (province of Santiago), San Vicente de Tagua–Tagua (province of O'Higgins), Chepica (province of Colchagua) and, more fleetingly, have made contact with various co-operatives in the provinces of Cautin, Llanquihue and Chiloë.

The choice of these places and organizations was partly pragmatic and partly based on theoretical sampling (see Glaser and Strauss, 1967). The choice was pragmatic insofar as it was backed up by good introductions and the possibility of obtaining these: whenever I arrived anywhere for the first time I always made sure to be equipped with a good introduction. The choice was theoretical insofar as it was based upon information concerning local circumstances or problems. In La Serena, for example, it was the personality of the young syndicate leader which greatly influenced my choice; in the province of Santiago the contrast between the poor, dry coastal region where the peasants proved easy to organize, according to my INDAP informants, and the region bordering on the big city where organization was said to be difficult. San Vicente was an area in which co-operatives in various stages of development were to be found, and where, in comparison with other regions, there existed a fairly close link between co-operative and syndicate. The local syndicate was, moreover, large and fairly strong. Chepica was one of the few co-operatives containing production groups who had land at their disposal. For that matter the entire province of Colchagua was interesting since it seemed that precisely here the peasants were deliberately engaged in bringing about a radical alteration of the agrarian structure. In Cautin, finally, I was particularly interested in the Mapuche reductions and the way in which the problem of the minifundia was being tackled at local level by the relevant government authorities.

2.2 The surveys

During the preliminary research I worked constantly at drawing up and refining hypotheses concerning affiliation and participation, for it was soon obvious that the presidential elections of September 1970 would cast their shadow so far before as to make it advisable to hold the surveys at a time when political passions would not yet have flared so high that every action was regarded as a political gambit. February, the last month of the holidays, appeared eminently suitable. Accordingly I began in December to work on the construction of a questionnaire, the appointment of interviewers and the selection of a sample.

For two reasons I decided against a random sample. Such a sample is only meaningful if one desires to generalize about the population from which it is taken. In explanatory and testing research, however, one frequently really generalizes about populations which are not limited in space and time (Philipsen, 1969, p. 19). This being so it seems better to chose cases in which the diversity of the universe finds expression. The population about which I wished to generalize, the peasants who might be members of a co-operative in Latin America, or even Chile, was so enormous that drawing a random sample would have entailed insurmountable difficulties. The same held good for the agricultural workers who might be members of a syndicate. In addition, I wanted to compare members with non-members who were working and living in the same natural circumstances or – in the case of the syndicates – dealt with the same owners. It seemed therefore a fairly obvious move to take members and non-members from the same community or the same enterprise. I thus interviewed 274 peasant producers, members and non-members of co-operatives, from the following seven communities: Cuncumen and Lo Abarca (Santiago province, Cuncumen Co-operative), Los Silos de Pirque, San José de la Estrella and Los Cañas (Santiago province, Brisas de Maipo Co-operative); Auquinco and Quinahue (Colchagua province, Chepica Co-operative). All the members in these communities were interviewed and one third of the non-member peasants – after I had obtained a list of the latter from those familiar with the local situation. These seven communities represent the contrast between the non-irrigated costal region and the irrigated central valley; between agriculture in really rural areas and farming carried on beneath the smoke of a city. They also show co-operatives in various stages of development and of varying viability. Cuncumen was one of the few co-operatives to be doing well economically and which could also avail of good management. Brisas de Maipo was much less well conducted, being scarcely active, but it had received a large sum of capital credit from INDAP for a horticultural marketing project. As I have said already, Chepica was one of the few co-operatives to have as members communal production groups with land at their disposal.

In addition a total of 210 members and non-members of peasant syndicates were interviewed in nine enterprises. These were San Manuel (Syndicate Melipilla); Los Toros, El Peñon and Zeralda (Syndicate Puente Alto); Viña Vieja, Vinã de Tagua – Tagua, Pumaiten, Idahue Norte and Los Mayos (Syndicate San Vicente de Tagua – Tagua). The first two communities mentioned are situated in the province of Santiago; San Vicente lies in the province of O'Higgins.

In all these farming enterprises a considerable section of the workers was not or was no longer organized. These farms were generally among the most prosperous; irrigation was

14

practised on all of them, but crop patterns differed. San Manuel grew wheat and kept dairy cows; the enterprises in Puente Alto went in for viniculture while those in San Vicente had fruit and tillage in addition to the vines. All three syndicates belonged to those founded by INDAP and were members of the confederation El Triunfo Campesino, at that period the largest in Chile. All three were also fairly efficient. On the enterprises mentioned all members were interviewed and half of those non-members who were in permanent employment. The respondents may thus be regarded as populations of which different sectors are compared (with each other). Although I shall approach my conclusions with caution, I am of the opinion, an opinion reinforced by the results of the anthropological research, that they are much more widely applicable.

The survey passed off well. There were practically no refusals – less than $\frac{1}{2}$%. It did admittedly prove difficult on some occasions to determine whether a person complied with the terms for being a respondent, notably whether a member of a co-operative could still be regarded as a farmer. In extremely doubtful cases I later removed the respondent; the number of such people amounted to about ten. On the conclusion of the survey the questionnaires were coded but not immediately punched and run off. I wished to get back as quickly as possible to the field research.

2.3 The anthropological field research

After the survey I took a closer look at one place, Cuncumen, to see how the co-operative fitted into the social structure. The intention was to gain some idea of what I had missed by the method I had employed hitherto – the gathering of incidents, particularly at meetings.

A second problem was that of solidarity in associations. Although it had become clear that the most important motive for affiliation was the hope of improving one's own personal, economic lot, it was equally clear that, given the co-operatives' lack of means and the divisions among the small farmers and the agricultural workers, the peasant movement could not get off the ground without a large measure of solidarity among a number of members at least.

I had in the meantime come to view solidarity not as a quality which a person either possessed or did not, but as an attitude which he displayed towards one group and not, or to a lesser extent, towards another. I was therefore primarily interested not in who felt solidarity towards their syndicate or co-operative and who did not, but in how that solidarity grew or could be made to grow.

The best way of discovering this might perhaps be to try oneself to induce this solidarity. Since this was impossible I selected various approaches, namely:

– attending, as a participant observer, courses which were intended to increase solidarity;
– interviews with peasant leaders and others who might be regarded as working in one way or another to increase solidarity;
– seeking out the differences between associative groups some of which appeared solidary and some of which did not (in this connection I concentrated on production groups, i.e. asentamientos and groups provided with credit by INDAP). I also coached two of my students during a five month stay in asentamientos in Aconcagua province where they investigated the acceptance of this communal enterprise and its

functioning in practice. I was able to use their notes on these assentamientos for this book (they have since been published in de Ranitz & de Ranitz, 1972);
– analyzing those incidents relating to solidarity which were provided by the meetings I continued to attend.

Before the end of my stay in Chile I wrote a first version of what, in this book, is the last chapter. This in itself proved a useful exercise; the concept of solidarity is so complicated that it helps to be obliged from time to time to marshal one's thoughts on paper.

In the third place, I spent the last months examining the factors which played a role in the structures and institutions surrounding the local community. These factors seemed of particular importance with regard to the co-operatives which were too weak financially to develop entirely under their own steam. The small farmers accepted the co-operative if it seemed economically successful and embarked on viable projects. I therefore paid particular attention to the expertise of the peasant leaders and of INDAP. I examined chiefly the leaders of the federation of Colchagua – the organizational zeal and consciousness of leaders appeared less advanced in other provinces, even though federations existed everywhere. Concerning INDAP I investigated several places where large projects were in train. Within this framework – but also in order to see whether affiliation and solidarity were perhaps influenced by other factors – I devoted the last month of my stay to a trip south, where I visited various associations on the island of Chiloë and in the provinces of Llanquihue and Cautin.

I relinquished my original plan to hold a second survey to find out what structural factors at local community level determined the degree of affiliation. This was because the political situation rendered further surveys inadvisable and also because the technical execution would have proved difficult and time-consuming. Instead, I collected data, for each community, on the degree of organization of the agricultural workers into syndicates, on the extent to which CORA had taken over enterprises and on the agrarian structure as revealed in the agricultural census of March 1965. After my return to the Netherlands these data were arranged and transferred to punch cards.

During the anthropological part of my research I proceeded with great caution. I did not want to run the risk of being accused of espionage, either by the right or by the extreme left. This caution led me to confine myself to one of the three national confederations of syndicates, namely El Triunfo Campesino, the confederation with which the government body which usually introduced me – INDAP – had the most dealings. I did not approach the other two; the communist – socialist confederation – Ranquil – because I only obtained sufficiently good introductions at a late stage and even then had the feeling that it would cost me too much time to gain the confidence necessary if I were to do what I wished to do, and the Catholic confederation – Libertad – I avoided because it was rumoured to work with American, even CIA money and I did not wish to lay myself open to gossip from leftist quarters. What now were the consequences of this voluntary limitation which on hindsight might be said to have sprung from an excessive degree of caution? Regarding the behaviour of the peasants I think that it had hardly any consequences at all. Many of my informants assured me that there was no difference between the confederations at the level of the members. I should have liked to learn a little more about the way in which Ranquil in particular set about indoctrinating its members. How did it manage to reconcile the apparently democratic election of local leaders with

16

the discipline which was at the same time demanded of these leaders? However, this gap did not affect the validity of what I did manage to discover.

2.4 My own values

A person's frame of reference determines to a large extent what he sees and how he interprets what he sees. Certainly now that in recent years the opinion is being voiced, that a great deal of social-scientific research which purports to be objective is in reality based upon a particular ideology – often conservative – it would seem sensible to try to set out my values explicitly here. The reader will then be in a better position to judge the contents of this book.

This is by no means a confession. Suffice it to say that certain experiences during my adolescence have inspired me with an aversion to propaganda and dogmatism, from whatever side. I have never been a member of a church or a political party. With regard to the churches, it is my conviction – which I will not elaborate – that they stifle man's religious feeling, that is to say his ability to construct a personal relationship with nature and with God. The very nature of the association with its inherent social control over the content of what one believes makes this unavoidable. As regards politics, I was fairly conservative when I went to Chile. This was not, I think, because I had any economic interests; my main interest, as an intellectual, is the freedom to publish my opinion. In Europe those countries in which the socialist revolution has taken place, have a bad reputation on this point. I was repelled by the lack of intellectual freedom, the double talk aimed at intellectual infants which streamed out of the Eastern European countries before the Czechoslovakian spring of 1968, by the dogmatism and the glorification of Marx expressed by many of those who, in the west, call themselves Marxists. All this seemed to me to be irretrievably bound.up with socialism as such. I find myself completely in agreement with the opinion of Deutscher, Coletti and many others – whom I only began to read after my return from Chile – that the Marxism which gained power in Russia has actively contributed to blocking the progress of socialism elsewhere in Europe.

Even in Brazil, where I worked from 1962–1965, in surroundings where I encountered few leftist colleagues, I found the 'left' rather hollow, with the exception of a couple of extremely intelligent people such as Caio Prado. Marxist theory seemed to suggest that the revolution (the real, not the bourgeois one) was imminent, while proving rather useless at analysis. At the end of their books many authors had conjured up ten classes or more instead of only two. It was with a certain wry pleasure that I tried to show, in 'Class and following in rural Brazil' that the peasants also availed of patronage in their mobilization or, to put it in Marxist terms, their class struggle (Galjart, 1964). This article has come under criticism from several colleagues (Huizer, 1965; Quijano, 1967). I believe now that I did wrong, in my impatience with the terms class and class struggle, which carried teleological nuances that helped to conceal from others the patronage mechanism in the peasant movement, to deny, not the existence of a conflict, but its character as a class struggle. Yet I believe too that I was acutely aware of reality at that time. I came to realize, during this 'conservative' period in Brazil, that peasants can only achieve communal development through co-operation, and that patronage was an obstacle to this co-operation. I took with me from Brazil part of the problem which I was later to investigate in Chile: upon what does solidarity among peasants depend?

In 1965 I returned to the Netherlands and a year later took up a position with the Department of Rural Sociology of the non-western regions in the Agricultural University. I mention this, because my contact with the students who, a short while later, revived their confrontation activities was important to me. I noticed that I could relate to them on an equal footing, and I was glad of this. Their politics were leftist, sometimes dogmatically so, but they were not politicians who had to keep up their position regardless. Contact with them has made me more 'leftist' on the one hand and on the other strengthened my impatience with and aversion to dogmatism. The world is grey and I think that it is especially important that idealists should realize this.

Chile proved to be not automatically comparable with Brazil. It was further developed, economically, but at the same time the limit of development offered by capitalism seemed to have been more or less attained. I made friends, especially in the circles of the leftist Christian-Democrats, the Mapu, who at this time had already broken away. I saw that they were serious-minded, worked hard and retained their critical faculties even with regard to their political allies on the left. This latter was extremely important, for in Chile too the left was vociferously dogmatic and believed its own propaganda and half truths. Important too was the fact that I saw the ideal in action and how some peasants reacted to it and gave of their utmost. I heard tales of the past, of the injustice done to them or their forefathers by some uncaring landed proprietor. I was disturbed by the lack of sensitivity, the absence of any fellow feeling for their poorer compatriots among the members of the élite with whom I came into contact in Santiago. In addition I saw that Chile was left with little choice: an agrarian development like that in Western Europe with a constant exodus of the less successful peasants towards other sectors of the economy was impossible there since the job opportunities were lacking. If agriculture was given the function of keeping people on the land a certain measure of equality would have to be created, and a redistribution of the land into family enterprises seemed less recommendable.

Thus, both intellectually and emotionally, I veered towards the left during my stay in Chile. How far? To some of my Chilean friends, to whom I then expressed my fear that in Chile too a dogmatic and authoritarian government by civil servants would succeed any eventual revolution, I am probably a half 'momio'; to Dutch friends, themselves half momios, I must appear as an extreme leftist, hairy sociologist. I do not really feel at home in either camp and count among my friends people who are prepared to see the person behind the ideology.

Perhaps though, this position is a valuable one after all. I hope to put it to use by acting as interpreter: here in the West I can explain the reasons behind the swerve to the left in underdeveloped countries; in those countries I may perhaps serve as a scientific conscience. It seems to me that the basis of all plans must be as objective an analysis of reality as possible. For this reason a scientific worker who acts as a restraining influence upon his colleagues who may be carried away by their ideological enthusiasm, may prove helpful. I know that a doubter like myself does not bring about a revolution, but to the necessary fanatics in the Third World I should like to say: have your revolution but when it is over learn to listen even to the doubters. No account is taken in this book, written between 1970 and 1973, of the Chilean attempts to achieve a socialist society. The implicit dialogue is with the government of the Unidad Popular, not with the men who now hold power. The dialogue deals with the organization of peasants into co-operatives and the degree to which certain socialist convictions, for example those relating to the 'new man', may lead to that organization being set up in a manner which in my opinion would be undesirable if the hoped for goals are to be attained.

The military coup of September 1973 has, for the time being, detracted from the relevance of my arguments, at least so far as Chile is concerned. This does not mean, however, that the book has been overtaken by events. What peasants want, what they do, why they band together and co-operate, and why they do not, all these are questions which remain relevant for the whole of the Third World, and a sociologist who attempts to answer some of them remains relevant too. Indeed it seems to me that the tragic course of events in Chile proves how difficult it is, in terms of national mobilization and the reaching of a consensus, to create a somewhat more just and human society. It is therefore still useful to know how peasants view such an attempt, even though they may seem less influential than other categories.

Chapter 3   The mobilization of peasants in Latin America: Approach to a theory

3.1   Definition and brief description

Mobilization is the process whereby social units – whether individuals or groups – are led to expend an amount, and sometimes a large amount, of the resources at their disposal: time, money, energy, enthusiasm, in order to attain a goal which they share with other units. Mobilization is thus the transfer, towards a new destination, by individuals or groups of resources previously used for their own ends. This transfer usually occurs fairly suddenly. Mobilization will take place when individuals are unable to bring about a desired situation by their own efforts. They are then confronted with the choice, either of attempting to do so together or of abandoning hope entirely.

In this chapter we shall discuss the *obstacles* to mobilization which peasants encounter in the social structure and in their own culture. We shall also deal with the *conditions* under which this mobilization may occur. In a later chapter, devoted to solidarity, we shall discuss the *problems arising after mobilization*, with reference to the permanent allocation of resources in favour of the new structures of collaboration.

Our definition implies that mobilization is a concept which must only be used for a particular goal or set of similar goals (cf. Etzioni, 1968, p. 420). In other words it is only when social units turn their efforts to the same goal that they can be said to be undergoing the same mobilization process. It appears from the literature and from the results of my own research which will be dealt with in the following chapters, that peasants mobilize primarily for reasons of self-interest. To put it in somewhat more general terms, they mobilize in the prospect of local objectives. They wish to achieve a desired situation for themselves, for their own locality. This is so both because peasants' interests are of a local-territorial nature and because mobilization assumes contact and interaction.

I shall begin therefore by analyzing, in model form, the extent to which Latin American peasants share, or do not share, the same interests. After this my argument will focus upon those peasants having a local opponent or opponents. The obstacles to and conditions for the mobilization of these peasants can be distinguished in a sketch like the one given below.

	local community	national society
STRUCTURAL OBSTACLES	Sections 3 + 5	Section 4
CULTURAL OBSTACLES	Section 6	Section 4

The squares contain the numbers of the sections of this chapter in which the relevant problems are dealt with.

Whether a group of peasants will attempt to and succeed in vanquishing a local opponent depends upon a large number of factors. At the present time it will be true to say that almost everywhere there is a considerable degree of economic and political incorporation of local communities into larger (regional and national) economic and political systems. This being so, the peasants' local opponent has economic and political allies to fall back on, including in the last instance, the State which can, and usually will, protect him with all the powers at its disposal. This in its turn means that a purely local peasant mobilization has little chance of success. Only mobilization on a national or regional scale whereby the peasants too seek allies in other economic and political sectors is likely to succeed. We shall thus be obliged to include in our discussion those structural and cultural changes which lead, on a national level, to a weakening of the position of the landed proprietors and a strengthening of that of the peasants.

It will be noted that the aggregation of interests which occurs when peasants mobilize at the national level leads to a fairly vague definition of objectives. Generally speaking it will be the State again which defines in detail the future picture of agrarian productive organization. Another factor which plays an important role in determining the success of mobilization on the local level, is the extent to which the peasants are able to rid themselves mentally of (the need for) a particularistic relationship with a patron. In situations of inequality, patronage is an almost ubiquitous redistribution mechanism which turns peasants into competitors and keeps them divided.

A fourth factor is entirely inherent in peasant culture, and derives from certain values and attitudes developed in a situation of oppression lasting many generations. These can make co-operation exceedingly difficult.

3.2 Kinds of local interests: a model

We shall begin by determining to what extent Latin-American peasants (campesinos) share the same aims[1]. For, after all, the term campesinos covers categories which have a different access to the means of production. It is possible to distinguish at least five such categories. In the first place there are the small owners and 'squatters' who have more or less independent possession of land upon which they run family farms which may or may not be large enough to supply their own needs. Secondly there are the tenants and sharecroppers who lease land from others against some form of payment but retain a degree of independence on how it is farmed. Thirdly, we have the colonos or inquilinos, peasants who spend the greater part of their time working for a landowner and receive in exchange, whether or not in addition to wages, the use of a small piece of land on which to grow food for themselves and their families. Fourthly, there are the permanent wage-labourers who work full-time for other people and are paid in cash, and fifthly, the temporary workers who are also paid in cash but are only employed for a certain period.

A first distinction of these categories is necessary, but not yet sufficient for an understanding of the mobilization process. It is necessary because, as will be come clear later on, these categories do not have exactly similar interests and may thus aspire to different goals. Usually they do not join the same organizations. In Brazil, during Goulart's time, the famous Ligas Camponesas directed by Julião, focussed their attention

Table 1. Paradigm of links between structural and cultural patterns in peasant communities

Basic hypothesis	Hypotheses regarding result	Categories of peasants	Hypotheses regarding maintenance of distribution	Hypotheses regarding resulting values and attitudes	Hypotheses regarding solidarity	Hypotheses regarding mobilization	Hypotheses regarding agricultural development
There will be rivalry among individual households for the possession of land	A. within the territory of the group there is considerable equality in the distribution of resources	in general small owners	strong levelling mechanisms of a legal, magic or ritual nature exist	strict social control	strong internal solidarity based on norms having a religious foundation; strong group solidarity in the face of threats from outside	interests: those of producers (prices, credit, market); mobilization for group interest hindered by levelling mechanisms	social control frustrates innovators since community is also reference group, little relative poverty, few needs; would-be innovators regarded as deviant; if more emerge group solidarity will decline
	B. within the territory of the group there is a certain degree of inequality in the distribution of resources	owners, small and larger; sporadically also tenant-farmers, sharecroppers and labourers	both levelling and suppression mechanisms occur; patronage (mechanism fulfilling both functions)	weak social control	internal solidarity on the basis of reciprocity and patronage; weak group solidarity in the face of threats from outside; status groups	interest: that of producers (not all to the same degree); smaller groups may have interest in redistribution; given heterogeneous nature of interests mobilization of community as a whole difficult	group resistance to further innovations slight; inequality will increase with development

C. Resources completely or almost completely monopolized by one or more large landowners; remaining households do or do not form a separate group with or without their own territory; within these the distribution of property or the use of resources can display a great measure of equality	community of owners of (sub) family farms surrounded by large land holdings, or of tenant farmers, sharecroppers or workers on large estates	levelling mechanisms within the group; patronage in relationships with landowners and the outside world; also suppression mechanisms	transition, depending upon the cohesion of the group of the remaining households, from strong social control based on communal values, to control based upon envy and mutual distrust; Image of Limited Good; growing escapism	transition, according to the cohesion of the group of the remaining households, from strong group solidarity in the face of threats from outside and towards monopolists to weak solidarity; similarly transition from strong internal solidarity to solidarity on the basis of dyads and kinship and to atomistic community	interests: 1. redistribution of resources and/or incomes therefrom; 2. those of producers; mobilization of the group of remaining households as a whole more difficult according as the group is more differentiated and less close-knit; depends upon weakening of patronage relationships and development of class-consciousness	group too poor to run risks of adoption; social control to prevent inequality may frustrate adoption; needs and relative poverty do exist; provided the group of the remaining households is still close-knit, community development projects are indicated

primarily on the first two categories (Moraes, 1970, p. 467); it was more usual for the workers to become members of rural syndicates. In Chile, during the time of Frei's government, by far the majority of rural trade union members belonged to the third and fourth categories; the temporary workers were scarcely organized at all.

However, another distinction must be made, based on the local distribution of the main resource, land, in the community or territorial unit in which the peasants are located. Upon this distribution depends the likelihood of the peasants' having a local opponent, a local conflict of interests. As Coser (1956, p. 34 and 90) has pointed out, the existence of a negative reference group is important for the formation of new groups. Conflict with a negative reference group will promote the internal cohesion of the peasants. A macro-sociological view which postulates that a conflict exists for the country as a whole, but which does not examine local conditions is in my mind too loose to explain the mobilization process. It is precisely the instigation of a local action, the existence of a local conflict, which often leads to full-scale mobilization, and this action depends upon the existence of local opponents. The macro viewpoint tends to assume a unity among peasants which is at best problematic and certainly cannot be taken for granted. On the other hand it does suggest, and rightly so, that ultimately a certain community of interests exists and that therefore the peasants will strive after unity.

By way of hypothesis, I assume that certain attitudes, values and mechanisms are linked with the local distribution of the means of production which has often existed unchanged for a very long time[2]. The possible distributions with their associated cultural elements are given in the model on pages 22–23. The basis is, as we have said, the local distribution of land. The model also contains assumptions regarding the mechanisms and values which help to preserve this distribution, once achieved, and regarding the interests and objectives at which the peasants will aim once mobilized. It must be stressed here that the model comprises ideal types and not descriptions. In reality elements from various ideal types can be found in one concrete locality. Minifundistas of type A may for example work as labourers upon the surrounding farms, giving rise to type C. The sharecroppers in C may form a separate ethnic group with strong mutual solidarity, so that the situation comes to resemble that of type A from a cultural point of view. Tenant farmers and sharecroppers may be found in B and even workers on the somewhat larger enterprises; it is, moreover, possible that as time goes by the distribution in B becomes more unequal, giving rise to a situation which has a great deal in common with C. In certain cases a large enterprise may be organized in such a way as to contain both sharecroppers and wage workers. Yet even though the reality is often difficult to classify, it seems to me that the model I employ may serve to bring a certain degree of conceptual order into the chaos of appearances.

One important distinction suggested by the model is that between situations in which one may speak of a local monopolization of land and thus of a clear conflict of interests (C) and situations in which this is not, or hardly the case (A and B). In C the mobilization of the dependent peasants will be aimed at the landed proprietors. Doubtful cases may also occur. Situation A may sometimes arise between the large estates, for instance in the higher sections of a catchment area, in the form of communities of small, independent peasants, to which the surrounding landed proprietors do not belong. If one examines the river basin as a whole the distribution of the land is very unequal, but locally, within such a community, the distribution may be comparatively fair. It is my hypothesis that a cultural pattern develops which is determined both by the relative local equality and by the inequality existing in the wider area[3].

The difference between one Indian peasant community possessing a reasonable acreage although surrounded on all sides by haciendas (situation A) and another Indian community which has too little land since it has lost part of it to the surrounding haciendas (situation C) is one of degree. In such a situation the course taken by mobilization will depend in the first place upon whether or not peasants include the land owned by the surrounding enterprises in their assessment of the local distribution. In other words, are these surrounding landed proprietors for them a negative reference group of land usurpers or do they leave them entirely out of their calculations? In the first case there is a conflict of interests within this type A community, while in the second case there is not. Indian communities of type A are seldom unaware that the surrounding landed proprietors have appropriated land which formerly belonged to them; they thus indeed regard them as opponents. Sometimes too we can speak of a conflict of interests when the inhabitants of a community of type A or B also work for part of the year as labourers or colonos upon a neighbouring enterprise (cf. Cotler, 1970, p. 60).

We shall now discuss in particular the mobilization of peasants against the landed proprietors, that is, situation C and, where relevant, A included in C. It is in such situations that the inequality, the social injustice is the most glaring. In these situations too mobilization most clearly assumes the character of a fierce political struggle – sometimes even carried on by force of arms. It is the outcome of this struggle which promises to have the most far-reaching consequences for the future development of Latin America, both rural and urban. Nevertheless we must point out that situations such as those we call C are not the only ones to occur. Millions of peasants live in situations which more closely resemble A or B. Mobilization against the landed proprietors ignores, in part at least, the interests of the peasants in such situations[4].

At a later stage, when the peasants in situations A and B have become more politicized and class conscious, and base their activities upon a view of the agrarian structure in a much larger area, their mobilization too may turn against a propertied class. In the first instance, however, their aim will be to defend those interests dear to them as independent producers.

3.3 Local, structural obstacles to mobilization

The model assumes that in C there is not a lone question of a conflict between those who monopolized the land and those who have little or none, but also of mechanisms intended to preserve the existing distribution and of cultural patterns which indicate an adaptation to this situation. The mechanisms referred to here are *coercion* and *patronage*. Coercion shows itself in: low wages, long hours of work, oral contracts for short periods, payment in coupons which can only be exchanged for goods in the store actually located on the hacienda, in the obligation to provide extra services which are often not paid for, in the obligation to sell agricultural produce through the owner, in dishonest practices with weights and measures, in the control exercised over the social contacts of peasants living on the property, and in the reprisals taken against those who were in any way rebellious. In some countries and at certain periods the owner had at his disposal a troop of armed henchmen whose task was not only to protect him against his equals but also to keep 'order' on his property. Since the introduction of formal, democratic election processes in the Latin-American countries the landed proprietors have tried in every possible way to persuade those peasants who are dependent upon them to cast their vote for the candidate of their (the landlord's) choice. Here too, if it proved necessary, that is to say if other means seemed likely to prove ineffective, coercion was used in the form of threats and reprisals (cf. Petras & Zeitlin, 1970, p. 510).

A much more subtle mechanism which helped to maintain the existing distribution was patronage. Patronage is an institutionalized relationship based upon an agreement, usually informal, between two persons (or parties) who differ in the degree to which they can influence the allocation of goods and services. The agreement implies that the one with the most influence, the patron, will use it in favour of the other party, the client, who will perform various services in return. According to Weber (1925, p. 681 ff.) the seed of this structural principle must be sought in the Oikos, the patrimonial property upon which a lord had power over the other members of a household, whether related to him or not. It is generally known that land in Latin America was usually given out in very large parcels; those who received land in this manner were sometimes able to avail at the same time of certain services from Indians living on the land or in the neighbourhood. Sometimes they had to see to the supply of workers themselves. The methods employed, such as slavery, debt bondage or the extreme monopolizing of the land by a few owners (cf. Pearse, 1970, p. 17), all led equally to the agrarian workers becoming extremely dependent upon the owner. In other words the agrarian structure which Weber regarded as the breeding ground of patronage existed in many places in Latin America. Patronage relationships, however, are also encountered between people who do not live on the same property, but who differ in status. Our model assumes that patronage will occur whenever an unequal distribution of land can be said to exist within an agrarian community. This hypothesis is based on the view that in such cases patronage can fulfil a useful function for both parties. The favour of the higher-ranking party, the surrender of goods or of the disposal of future goods, is 'exchanged' for the service of the lower ranking party which consists in acknowledging the prestige and legitimate authority of the other. A somewhat greater economic equality is obtained at the expense of greater social and political inequality. The higher-ranking person can use his legitimated power to promote, either directly or indirectly, his appropriation of economic goods.

One important aspect of patronage is that it is not a relationship which springs up automatically between a rich landowner and a poor peasant. Its inception depends upon the quality of the personal relationship between the two participants; it also assumes personal loyalty on the part of one towards the other. The person in the lower position places himself under the protection of the person in the higher. Usually the initiative for embarking upon the relationship comes from the lower placed person; in most cases he has more to gain than the other. For someone who already enjoys the prestige of a number of dependents, the increase in prestige which he gains by accepting a new client is slight. The fact that the initiative usually comes from the person of lower status has been directly observed (Galjart, 1968, p. 86; Hutchinson, 1966; Williams, 1969, p. 88) but it is also apparent from the tendency which occurs in differentiated communities to acquire persons of higher status as ritual co-parents, potential patrons (see Mintz & Wolf, 1967, p. 195). Although it is true that patronage has yet another, latent, function which may benefit the patron, Huizer's suggestion (1970, p. 22 and 188) that it is the patron who seeks to establish the patronage relationship must be regarded as incorrect.

This latent function of patronage, one that is very important with regard to mobilization, is that it keeps the dependent peasants divided. They are rivals for a patron's favours. In an earlier piece of research undertaken in Brazil (Galjart, 1968, p. 86) I viewed the lack of horizontal solidarity among peasants of equal social status as forming part of their tendency to seek patronage relationships. Cotler (1969, p. 65) indicated the same phenomenon for Peru when he called the pattern of social relationships of dependent peasants a 'triangle without a base'. Even though patronage certainly does not affect all, or even a majority of the potential clients – the peasants and labourers on a property – and even though only a few profit by a good relationship with the patron, this does not detract from the cultural influence of the institution. It helps to keep those individuals who seek patronage apart from the majority and thus harms their solidarity. In this way it fulfils for the patron a useful role of divide and conquer and achieves this so effectively precisely because it does, on occasion, offer a person of lower status the possibility of vertical mobility. One frequently finds that the supervisory – and better paid – personnel on the large agricultural enterprises originate from the category of agricultural workers. Certainly it is only a small percentage of the agrarian population which can better itself in this manner, but equally certain is the fact that their example helps to keep alive a belief in the effectiveness of patronage in much wider circles.

The increasing, almost obligatory openness of the local agrarian community or the hacienda, the growing influence of the central government and state institutions upon local events has not led automatically to the disappearance of patronage. On the contrary, the mechanism has been strengthened rather by the introduction of elections and of suffrage. The patron, belonging as he did to the local élite which enjoyed power and prestige, could, if he wished, take on another function. He could become the intermediary between the central government apparatus and the local community. He could do this either by entering politics himself, or by initiating patronage relationships with influential persons in the comprehensive systems. The function of 'broker' has already been described by many authors (including Wolf, 1956; Dandler, 1969; Pascal, 1968). This function need not necessarily be fulfilled by a landed proprietor, since the precondition is not ownership of land but the possession of relations and contacts with strategically placed persons in the outside world.

In any case it is a fact that the introduction of formal democratic political procedures has not curtailed the power of the landed proprietor. For a long period it has served rather to increase it. The client or potential client, the dependent peasant was put in a position to perform a valuable service for the patron, that of voting for the patron's candidate. In actual fact it was a long time before the peasant himself realized the true value of this service. Coercion and patronage both made it possible for the patron to dispose of the votes of those peasants dependent on him[5]. The result was that the owners of large estates were able to retain a considerable degree of political power for a long time, even where, from the national point of view, they were becoming less important as an economic force. In some countries they still do. A good example of this is what happened in Chile in 1939 (cf. Affonso *et al.,* 1970, I, Chap. 1). In spite of an election victory by the candidate of the popular front who had the support of the communist and socialist parties, the radical party was able to make its participation in the coalition government dependent upon the promise that the government would not tolerate syndicates of agricultural workers.

Despite the rise of political parties drawing their electorate principally from the urban proletariat and being also interested in the peasants' votes, the landed proprietors dominated these to such an extent that it was a long time before the parties got a foothold at all. Indeed, in some countries they have not managed to do so yet. The political power of these large property owners means that the State, with its machinery of repression, is on their side when it comes to frustrating the peasants' concrete attempts to mobilize. They are also able to have reforms of the agrarian structure postponed even where laws have been enacted to this purpose despite their opposition.

From what we have said thus far it becomes clear that even though the peasants mobilize to bring about a local redistribution of income or resources, the degree to which the local community and, notably, their opponents, the landed proprietors, are incorporated in the national political system, means that they have more to cope with than merely local opposition. Although the breaking down of the patronage relationship between landed proprietor and peasant remains one of the conditions for success of these attempts at mobilization, it is not the most important. This continues to be the smashing or at least the neutralizing of the landed proprietors' political power at national level. Several authors have suggested that reforms of the agrarian structure and the mobilization of the peasants only got under way after the large estate owners had already lost some of their power (cf. Moraes, 1970, p. 467 ff.; Chonchol, 1970, p. 33 ff.; Craig Jr., 1969, p. 292).

Before returning to the local level in order to determine under what conditions a weakening of patronage might be expected, we shall deal with the power of the landed proprietors within the national political and economic systems. Even there their power does not last for ever, although it has existed for centuries. The tragedy is, however, that the peasants themselves can contribute very little towards creating the conditions under which this power can be curtailed.

3.4 Structural and cultural conditions for peasant mobilization on the national level

It is true to say of most Latin American countries that for centuries the power of the landed proprietors has been chiefly local. In the absence of a strong central authority, the boundaries of their territory were at the same time the boundaries of a political unit which was to all intents and purposes independent. The greatest potential enemy of the landed proprietor was often another landed proprietor and there were frequent conflicts between them about land or other matters. This was tied up with the fact that the hacienda, no matter how large, was always potentially capable of further expansion (see Wolf & Hansen, 1966, p. 171). Local or regional alliances were also formed when it became necessary to promote a particular interest.

The landowners only began to act as a national interest group when the central authority became strong enough to start laying down the law to them on certain points. Their power within the national system was based upon three factors. In the first place there was their *economic* importance. In many countries they were the chief producers of export products and since a large part of the state income was derived from an export levy, they were also the most important tax payers. But even apart from this levy, the fact remained that the agrarian product accounted for a considerable share of the total national product and that the landed proprietors therefore earned a large part of the national income.

In the second place their power was *political* and based upon their domination of people. This applied not only to the dependent peasants on their own estates but also to those of smaller landowners in the neighbourhood and to the relatives, servants and other members of the household of all these people. Both during the time of the regional caudillos who fought among themselves to decide who would control the positions of central authority and later, when democratic elections took over the function of ousting the government in office, those who held the peasants' loyalty, held power. Although some of the caudillos were not of the landed proprietor class, many of them were, and in almost every Latin American country, until well into the twentieth century, the large landowners furnished many prominent politicians. In addition the power of the large landowners found expression in their control of a number of political parties, some of them extremely large, which succeded for a long time in blocking changes in rural areas through the actions of their parliamentary delegates. They managed, for instance, to hold up the extension to the rural areas of labour legislation. In this way too they were able to mobilize the armed power of the state for their own ends if by any chance some movement of revolt did break out. In such cases the police and the army were none too gentle in restoring order.

Their third power base was the actual interest group, the *lobby*, often called something like 'national society of agriculture'. Such a society strove not only to promote certain government measures which would be advantageous to its members, but also analyzed the possible consequences for agriculture of other measures and bills. If its analysis proved negative, it initiated resistance, often successfully. McBride (1970, p. 169) describes how the Chilean Sociedad Nacional de Agricultura, in a communication to the members of 1924, states that not alone has it put a stop to the radical movement among the workers but it has also prevented the construction of a railway over the Andes in the south of Chile which would have made it possible to import cattle on the hoof from Argentina and thus would have weakened the competitive position of cattle farmers living in southern Chile.

What factors have contributed or can contribute to a weakening of the power position of the large landowners or to neutralizing their power?

In my opinion the first to be mentioned must be the gradual growth of *industry* over the past forty years. This is based chiefly on import replacement and must therefore find an internal outlet in order to continue in existence. This leads one immediately to a basic contradiction; it is in the interests of industry, or at least of the producers of ordinary consumer goods, to have a farming population which earns enough to be able to buy its products. Industrialization in itself creates two new interest groups, the industrialists and the workers. Other processes of change, such as urbanization, the rise of a bureaucratic government apparatus and the emergence of middle classes to man the service sector, which may in part occur autonomously but which may also be caused by industrialization, also lead to the appearance of new interest groups. All this means, *ipso facto*, that the national product is no longer earned solely in agriculture, by the large landowners.

The basic conflict between industry and the surplus appropriation by the large land-owners remained for a long time submerged. It has, nonetheless, given rise to adaptations in the price relationships between industrial goods and agricultural produce which are disadvantageous to agriculture (cf. Evers & Vossenaar, 1971). In order to avoid a direct confrontation, industrialists and landowners have arrived at a sort of compromise; the absence of a home market is compensated for by high prices for industrial goods and stringent import restrictions. Ultimately, however, this has weakened the position of the landowners nonetheless. Deprived of incentives, agriculture was unable either to increase production and productivity to any great extent or to offer the peasants an existence more consistent with human dignity. This state of affairs was sometimes acknowledged by the landowners: in Chile it was one of the arguments with which the SNA tried to shift the blame from its members (Gomez, 1969, p. 83 ff). However, in a situation where for years arguments have been employed with the object of preventing, postponing or watering down reforms, no one pays attention any more to the truth content of an argument.

Industrialization thus has led in more than one way to a weakening of the economic power of the landowners. That this weakening favours peasant mobilization seems beyond dispute. When mobilization began in Chile in 1965, the agrarian population still formed at most 30% of the total. In addition the agriculturalists, that is to say, the landowners, had been discredited in the eyes of a broad section of the public (Chonchol, 1970, p. 56) by the fact that agriculture, which before the second world war had provided a foreign exchange surplus of some 40 million dollars, was so incapable of satisfying the demand for food in the sixties that an annual food import of 150 million dollars was necessary.

One might assume that the emergence of new interest groups which are beginning to take part in the political process and help to influence the allocation of public resources, will affect the political power of the landowners. This is indeed so, in a certain sense, but the process may at best be called devious. Insofar as one can speak of a democratically elected government, this can no longer be formed entirely by parties dominated by the landowners. It will have to be a coalition government. We have already seen, however, that even in these circumstances the landowners manage to preserve the status quo in the countryside for quite a long time by forming alliances or entering into agreements with other interest groups. They managed to preserve it for so surprisingly long in fact that it has given rise to a theory of political development having special reference to Latin America.

Anderson (1964) has postulated that, in the Latin American countries, every newly emerging interest group has to prove its power capability. This is then followed by admission to the political arena, provided that the sitting power groups are convinced that the newcomer will keep to the rules of the game. And, one of the main rules is that they will not eliminate any of the traditional power groups. Each group continues to participate. This 'theory' which is nothing else but an ideal typical description of what actually seems to take place in a number of countries implies that new groups, which often started out with very revolutionary ideas and slogans, are in a certain sense absorbed. They connive with the others to keep the system functioning and themselves become members of the élite. Several authors in fact (including Fals Borda, 1968, p. 67) speak of a workers' aristocracy. This 'theory' is important in relation to the peasants in that they are one of the few remaining collectivities which still have to prove their 'power capability' and thereby find themselves opposed to a system of interests which is already to a large extent differentiated.

In a certain sense all the other power groups will have to give way a little when the peasants finally begin to participate. Conversely, this also means that, despite all slogans to the contrary, the peasants cannot count on the urban workers as convinced political allies. However, this situation will not last indefinitely. Developments such as the extension of the franchise to illiterates[6], a considerable increase in the number of literates (who are entitled to vote) and reforms in the election procedures which will ensure that voting is really secret (and thus impossible for the owners to check up on) and fraud impossible, make it an attractive proposition for those parties not controlled or influenced by landowners, to seek voters in the rural areas. In this way a power ratio may finally emerge on the national level, within a coalition for example, such that a government will be reluctant to use repressive measures against the peasants, even if requested to do so by the landed proprietors and their allies in parliament[7].

It is also possible, however, that the large landowners will find political allies in those parties dominated by industrial interest groups and the middle classes. This can happen when the groups which champion agrarian reform also threaten the non-agrarian ownership of the means of production.

There can be no doubt that the State's reluctance to employ repressive measures is essential to peasant mobilization. The history of many Latin American countries is full of examples of dispersed jacqueries, vanished organizations, ill-fated actions on the part of the peasants. On the other hand it is frequently possible to detect government neutrality or even good-will underlying successful peasant actions. According to Craig Jr. (1969, p. 286), the more open policy of the Prado government in Peru towards new trade unions stimulated the setting up of the first of these organizations in the Convención valley. Syndicalization later received a welcome stimulus from a recommendation favouring the peasants which was made by a research commission of the Ministry of Labour, sent to the valley to investigate a conflict (idem, p. 288). Arroyo and Gomez (1969) have gathered data for Chile which show the enormous consequences resulting from the com-

Table 2. Number of conflicts in agricultural enterprises (Chile)

| Year | C.W.C.[1] | Strikes | Occupation of enterprises by | |
			Workers	Mapuche
1960	60	3	—	—
1961	12	7	1	1
1962	21	44	—	1
1963	10	5	—	2
1964	31	39	—	1
1965	395	142	7	6
1966	526	586	14	4
1967	1167	693	7	2
1968	1852	647	24	2

1. Collective wage contracts

ing to power of the Frei government i.e. a government well disposed towards trade un-
ionism. This was so even in the early years when the legislation remained unchanged,
being merely differently applied. Whereas before 1964 there were only about 20 rural
syndicates in existence, this number had grown to 201 by 1966 and to 394 by 1970. Table
2, derived from the same authors, shows that the number of actions also increased by
leaps and bounds during the period of Frei's government.

Peasant organizations themselves developed a number of tactics aimed at neutralizing
the power of the landed proprietors and increasing the government's reluctance to use
repressive measures. Firstly, in many countries they came to realize that local
organizations, acting alone, always lose a conflict. Even though their action usually
remains local, the organizations are in a stronger position if they unite in an umbrella
movement; their solidarity not only makes repression more difficult, but also more risky
for a government which ultimately depends upon winning elections.

In the second place one often finds (cf. Huizer, 1970) that the peasants start out by
making demands which amount merely to the application of an already existing law;
demands for the payment of a legal minimum wage, demands for the enforcement of the
legally prescribed hours of work, demands for the abolition of contractual obligations
declared invalid by law. Such tactics also make it more difficult for the government to act
repressively.

Thirdly the peasants – and later their organizations – seek allies among other population groups or else accept invitations to join alliances made to them by other groups or
persons. This scouting round for allies is evident in the first place from the fact that many
of the leaders of peasant organizations were not peasants themselves but had a higher
standing in the community as lawyers, priests or urban intellectuals. The name of the
lawyer Francisco Julião is linked with the famous Ligas Camponesas from Goulart's
period. In that same period the priests Crespo and Lage were well known leaders of the
syndical movement in north-eastern Brazil. Hugo Blanco, the man who helped organize
the peasants in the Convención Valley in Peru was a student of agriculture; Emilio Loren-
zini, who organized the first big strike of Chilean agricultural workers in 1953, was a
jurist and son of one of the local notables; Juan Cifuentes, who did the same thing a year
later in a neighbouring community, 'came from a family which had produced a long line
of bishops and ministers of state' (Landsberger, 1969, p. 223).

Through their higher social-economic status – and sometimes by virtue of family ties
with local notables – they are less easily 'got at' by the local landowners. The latter are
not quite sure what hornet's nest they may be stirring up if they try to take reprisals
against them, for they prefer to aim their reprisals at the local leaders of peasant
organizations. Even as late as 1965 it was difficult, in Chile, say Affonso et al. (1970 II, p.
236), to find peasants who were prepared to occupy any leading position in the syndicates. It is not surprising therefore that it is sometimes necessary to have an alliance
beforehand to get any local peasant organization going at all. In a large number of cases
the first impetus towards a local association must come from an outsider. Such an
organiser may be some socially aware person, like a priest or a student, or someone connected with a leftist political grouping, or even a civil servant (Chile); this depends on the
political circumstances.

The aim of such a mobilizer is frequently not merely to organize the peasants so as to be able to demand better living conditions. If he has political affiliations he will also be eager to gain support for his party or group; if he has a particular social ideal in mind, he will try to whip up the peasants' enthusiasm for it so that they will demand the necessary changes; if he himself has political ambitions he will want to win voters. Certainly, if the mobilizer is affiliated to an important party any alliance he sets in motion will serve several functions. It protects the peasants and serves as a channel for communication and negotiation with the national level on which decisions regarding the solution of conflicts are taken. For the government is not important merely as the possible tool of the landed proprietors. Even when it ceases to fulfil this role so obviously, it must still solve conflicts, take decisions regarding the allocation of resources and legalize any new measures. The government remains important to the peasants and so accordingly do good relations with this government and the channels of communication via which they may argue their case. For the political party any alliance with the peasants is intended to bind them to it[8]. The APRA in Peru, the MNR in Bolivia, A.D. in Venezuela, PRI in Mexico, FRAP and PDC in Chile were all familiar with such 'tied' peasant organizations. However, although in one case (Mexico) the peasants, once 'tied', received hardly any help from their party and in the other (Venezuela) it is doubtful whether, after a very promising start, the party now pays much attention to the peasants at all, there seem to be cases in which the party continued to support the peasant organizations (Peru, Chile). One seems justified in assuming that the support the peasants receive is directly related to the importance of their political support for those groups or organizations which hold power within the state or, conversely, to the threat which their opposition might pose to these power élites. In any case, such an alliance, which sometimes assumes the character of a client relationship, is one more example of the importance for the peasants of linking up with other groups.

One cultural factor which helps to weaken the power of the landed proprietors is ideological. It concerns the emergence, first among the urban intellectuals, and later among other population groups, of a set of related ideas and concepts which detract from the prestige of the hacendados.

The actual origin of these ideas seems to be connected with a question which began once again to pre-occupy Latin American intellectuals during the twenties. They started to ask themselves *why* their countries were under-developed. Previous generations had usually sought the answer in a supposed racial inferiority of the Indian or, as the case might be, black section of the population. Gradually, however, the stereotypes of the stupid, apathetic peasant, devoid of any culture of his own and incapable of creating one, became unacceptable (Quijano, 1965, p. 57). People began to regard the position of the dependent peasant, existing on the very edge of, or below, the subsistence level, as being contrary to all justice. In the first instance this led to an unfavourable view of the agrarian sector, which was considered traditional, clinging to out-of-date techniques and methods and to a social order in which the enterprising peasant was given no opportunity. At a later stage, during the fifties, people also began to attribute the stagnation in the economic development of society as a whole to the excessively stratified social structure obtaining in rural areas. This was seen as an obstacle not only to agrarian development, but also to industrial growth since it was accompanied by a lop-sided distribution of income which led to the absence of a large home market. To crown it all, the rich sections of the population, which included the large landowners, did not even fulfil those obligations entrusted to them earlier by the economists. In other words they neither saved nor invested. A luxurious life style and the flight of capital prevented this. It would lead us too far astray to examine these ideas in any more detail; suffice it is to say that they did and do exist and are expressed more and more frequently by very serious and respectable organizations such as the Economic Commission for Latin America (see Cepal, 1969, p. 28 ff.)[9].

These ideas, theories and facts led in their turn to divisions within what, for convenience sake, we will call the ruling élites and within the actual landed proprietor category. The more far-seeing, progressive and enterprising individuals and groups within these élites realized that it would be impossible to preserve the status quo in the rural areas much longer and that a timely attempt at reform could prevent later revolutionary outbursts. The United States too urged reforms in 1961. This at least resulted in most Latin American countries adopting some laws relating to land reform, although none of them seems to have been in much of a hurry to put these laws into execution. In some of the countries themselves several élite groups were prepared to drop the landed proprietors in order to save interests to which they attached more weight. It also hapened that the more progressive and productive land owners were quite prepared to accept a type of land reform which would spare them while penalizing their unproductive colleagues (Bourricaud, 1967, p. 297). Indeed the Chilean government deliberately made use of this differentiation between productive and unproductive estates in order to sow discord among the large landowners (McCoy, 1969, p. 19).

One other result has been that young people, especially students, were stimulated to activism. In various countries and at different periods they surged into the countryside bent on organizing the peasants, making them aware of their condition and spurring them to action. Their activities met with considerable success in some places (cf. Horne, 1971); elsewhere, where they embarked upon a guerilla struggle against the government and its army in the hope of carrying the peasants along with them, their effect remained slight.

In conclusion it may be stated that the peasants themselves can exercise only a minimal influence upon the creation of those conditions necessary to neutralize the power of the landed proprietors at the national level. Even when voting in elections and in seeking political allies, they depend upon the existence of parties, groups and persons willing to help them.

Now that we have reviewed at the national level the processes necessary for a successful mobilization of the peasants let us return to the local level. There we shall discuss what circumstances may contribute to a weakening of the patronage relationship between owner and peasants.

3.5 Factors leading to a weakening of the patronage relationship

That patronage relationships hamper peasant mobilization became very clear during our anthropological research in Chile. It was not infrequntly said of completely unorganized enterprises of any size that the owner 'bribed' his peasants. He found out what minimum wage the syndicate was demanding and then offered slightly more himself on the condition – either tacit or openly expressed – that the peasants should not organize. Under what circumstances now does this relationship between owner and peasant become more contractual and specific, embracing fewer facets of life?

In general we may expect this to happen whenever economic and agrarian *development* takes place within a district. There are several reasons for this. Economic development implies increasing differentiation and specialization of roles in economic life. This creates alternative outlets for the peasants, enabling them to break the link with the patron through individual migration. The very fact that such alternatives exist will already lessen their dependence. The incorporation of the local community into the national economic, political and cultural systems which is characteristic of development also results in the peasants making contact with authorities and dispensers of assistance other than the landowner alone, the regional representatives of various government bodies for instance. Even if these persons must still be approached through channels, people other than the owner will possess the necessary contacts.

In a diagram derived from Cotler (1969, p. 72) we might convey the accompanying change in the patronage relationships of the peasants as the transition from Fig. A to Fig. B. Brokerage occurs alongside feudal patronage (Blok, 1969).

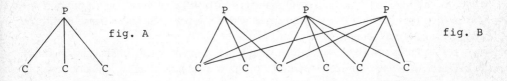

In a somewhat later stage of development the neighbourhood begins to offer the peasants all kinds of possible new roles such as parent of school-going children, market seller, adopter of some novelty, sportsman. Alberti (1970), working on a theory advanced by Young, analyzed three Peruvian farming communities and concluded that in these changed circumstances the peasants resent their complete dependence more than before and that, since this feeling is shared, solidarity among them grows.

Agrarian development on the farms themselves also leads to a differentiation and specialization of roles. The patron becomes dependent upon the special skills of some workers; his relationship with them becomes more impersonal, more contractual. It has been established that in several countries – Peru, Brazil, Chile – agrarian development leads to the traditional method of payment i.e. receiving the use of land, being replaced by payment in cash (cf. Cotler and Portocarrero, 1970, p. 133; Ramirez, 1969, p. 56). This phenomenon too renders the relationship more contractual. It often happens that the worker who receives payment partly or entirely in the form of land has a higher standard of living than his colleague who receives only money. On the farming enterprises in which both categories occur the first regards himself as the more privileged, which also means the more dependent upon the owner's favour.

Insofar as development also implies a higher income for the peasants, as was the case for example in the valley of La Convención in Peru, it also allows them a greater degree of independence from the landowners. In the valley the sharecroppers had earned so much from the coffee they grew on their land that they were able together, per hacienda, to enlist the services of a lawyer in order to lodge a complaint with the Ministry of Labour. Later they were even in a position to boycot the owners, that is, to refuse to work for them any longer either for money or any other inducement. It seems, however, that development of this sort, which arouses such expectations, must either be halted or menaces leaving them a prey to frustration, before a more radical mobilization of the peasants occurs (cf. Huizer, 1970, p. 185 ff.; Craig Jr., 1969, p. 285; and Lamond Tullis, 1970)[10].

Factors closely connected with development are the proximity of an *urban centre* and the presence of *educational facilities*. The urban centre helps to make the peasants aware of alternative opinions and possibilities of behaviour – a role which may nowadays be fulfilled to some extent by the transistor radio – and makes it easier for the mobilizers to reach them. Education can, in theory, increase their chances of detaching themselves from the patron individually and open their eyes to the existence of alternatives. Other factors which may be expected to contribute to a weakening of the patronage relationship relate to the individual farm or ranch. These are:

– The size of the enterprise. The larger the number of workers, the more difficult it is for the owner to embark upon a relationship of patronage with the majority. There is an increased likelihood that a considerable number will not feel any personal link with the owner at all.

In Chile it was often the smaller farms with only two or three workmen besides the owner, which were not syndicalized. Quijano (1965, p. 47) points out that the peasant unions in the Peruvian Sierra usually emerged where the population was dense and there were practically no medium-sized enterprises.

– Owner absenteeism. Even where the owner's replacement is an administrator and not an overseer who has risen from the ranks of the workers, he usually does not have the owner's liberty to dispense favours which cost money. He cannot thus maintain the patronage relationships. Moreover, it seems as though the administrators tend to exploit their position in order to grow rich as quickly as possible, to the disadvantage both of the owner and the workers. At least I frequently got this impression both in Brazil and later in Chile. Whenever the peasants' conversation came round to an administrator, it was remarkable how often they held a more unfavourable opinion of this man than of the owner himself.

— The rapid succession of owners. Patronage is a personal relationship and needs time in order to develop; the worker has first to prove that he is worthy of the landowner's trust. It would seem an obvious assumption – but this is a hypothesis which could only be illustrated by a few examples – that the sale of a farm, or its being inherited by another member of the family, would weaken the patronage relationships between peasants and owner.

Alongside factors relating to conditions in a particular region or enterprise one might also mention a number of others involving the experiences or characteristics of the peasants themselves. It may be assumed, for instance, that peasants with a couple of years experience of working in the towns or in the mines will be less inclined to an uncritical acceptance of patronage relationships with the owner of the agricultural enterprise on which they later find themselves working. Several authors mention the fact that in particular the leaders of peasant movements have undergone this kind of experience, which might be called *re-socializing* (Huizer, 1970, p. 181; Alberti, 1970, p. 187; Craig Jr., 1969, p. 268; Affonso *et al.*, 1970, 2, p. 227).

In areas with an Indian population partial or complete participation in the Latin culture and structure also forms part of this re-socializing experience (cf. Quijano, 1965, p. 59 f.).

The same effect might be expected of migration within agriculture itself as occurs when temporary agricultural labourers travel from one farm to another. Gilhodes (1970, p. 449) says that in Colombia it was largely from the landless wandering mass of agricultural workers that the participants in the armed conflicts, collectively called la violencia, emerged. On the basis of their ecological analysis of the results of the Chilean presidential elections of 1958 and 1964 Petras and Zeitlin (1970, p. 515) suggest that it will be the migratory seasonal workers, the afuerinos, who will be more inclined to perceive the common interests they share with other peasants and workers and to accept radical political explanations for their common situation.

Finally we must mention the possible role of a *particular event which* increases the peasants' frustration. These would include attempts on the part of the owners to alter conditions of work to their own advantage, the cancellation of favours previously granted or attempts to drive the peasants from their land (cf. Alberti, 1970, p. 211). It is not only their increasing frustration but also the fact that the peasants can hold no one but the landowner responsible for this frustration which makes them ripe for mobilization.

In this section we have mentioned a number of concrete factors which in our view contribute to a weakening of the patronage relationship. In the following chapter we shall examine, in the light of quantitive data relating to Chilean rural municipalities, what confirmation we can find for the series of hypotheses developed here.

We shall now turn to a discussion of the cultural obstacles to mobilization and the conditions under which these may be removed.

3.6 Obstacles to mobilization present in the local culture and their possible removal

From the model presented earlier it may be deduced that also *cultural* obstacles to mobilization may exist. The model in fact postulates that there will be a connection between the local distribution of land and the occurrence of a number of culture patterns other than patronage. While patronage is, in a certain sense, an implicit acceptance of the inequality which lies behind it, some quite different reactions to this inequality exist. Röling (1970) assumes that peasants who are unable to carry through an innovation for whatever reason may try to work out their frustration in various ways. In agreement with Merton he mentions rebellion, escapism, ritualism and conformism and adds the creation of controlling forces. We may regard the century-long inability of the majority of the Latin American agrarian population to better their position in life as the impossibility to create a particular desired situation. We may then expect that this population group will have to work out the consequent frustrations in some way or another. It makes sense to regard what Huizer (1970) calls 'the culture of repression' as inbuilt adaptations to this frustration.

The literature dealing with Latin American peasant cultures contains descriptions of elements which would fit very nicely into one of Röling's rubrics. The widespread drunkenness, for instance, could be classed under escapism as could the apparent laziness, the apathy, the lack of foresight. There is also the belief, so widespread in Brazil, in the 'golpe', the stroke of good luck needed to succeed. This would come under the crea-

37

tion of controlling forces. Under ritualism one might mention the striving after satisfaction of ritual obligations instead of wealth as described by van Zantwijk (1965, p. 166 f.) writing of an Indian village in Mexico. Rebellion would cover not only the countless jacqueries which have occurred in Mexico, Peru and other countries but also the emergence of what has been called social banditry[11].

There can be little doubt that the kinds of adaptation to frustration mentioned by Röling occur frequently in the rural areas of Latin America. However, only a few of the authors who describe any of these forms of cultural adaptation give sufficient information concerning the local distribution of land to be able to 'place' the various cultural patterns in our model. Then again, other cultural traits such as the peasants' mistrustfulness, which has been remarked upon by many, seem not to fit very well into any of Röling's categories. Williams too (1969) in a research conducted with Peruvian peasants, has attempted to detect psychosocial characteristics which might have resulted from their being dominated for generations by the landed proprietors[12]. He mentions the tendency to avoid taking decisions; to approach the outside world with rough and ready dichotomic concepts such as friend and enemy, ignoring, as it were, the more subtle nuances in attitude; a lack of tolerance for vagueness and ambiguity; an orientation towards present or past but not towards the future over which the peasant has no control, fatalism, in other words; and the active solicitation of patronage.

All these examples, to which may be added the envy and social control already mentioned, indicate that the agrarian structure in Latin America has led in many parts to the formation of more or less stable cultural patterns which will influence the success of any eventual attempts at mobilization and even the acceptance of new social structures. We still know little about the way in which cultural patterns change. It would be mistaken to think, however, that even where a cultural trait has originated as a result of a particular structure, the cultural pattern in question will automatically disappear with any later structural change. It is also certain that the mobilization of the peasants will itself have to overcome the resistance of such dysfunctional culture patterns.

What factors may help to neutralize and overcome cultural obstacles such as the mutual mistrust, the lack of solidarity, the tendency to interpret a person's actions in terms of self-interest, to regard the non-related other as a rival in the struggle to grasp at least a share of life's limited opportunities? Insofar as the peasants still form a certain community and do not live completely atomistically within a geographical area, the *threat from outside* is an important factor in promoting solidarity. This threat may come from a traditionally negative reference group from which the peasants differ radically. In such cases the community will often preserve a certain show of unity no matter how divided it may be on the inside. This mixture of inward division and the presentation of a united front towards outsiders is not infrequently found in Indian communities. The peasants may also be made aware of the existence of a threat by a particular event, disadvantageous to them all, or by the stimulating effect of messages emanating from external agents.

The campaign against adult illiteracy was used in Brazil at the beginning of the sixties (cf. de Kadt, 1970) and later in other countries, to help promote this awareness by using texts which explained, in terms of power and class, the situation in which the peasants found themselves. In the San Miguel Valley in the Peruvian Andes, eleven of the eighteen

Indian communities, some lying inside and some outside a large hacienda, united in a federation when taxation on their land was instituted (Diaz, 1970). On the fundo Pullally in Chile a similar event, which was to everyone's disadvantage, was the refusal of the patron to rebuild at his expense houses which had been partially destroyed by an earthquake. This led to the sharecroppers and the overseers, with their higher incomes, becoming members of the syndicate (de Ranitz and de Ranitz, 1972).

One other factor which promotes solidarity is the *project*, the aiming towards some particular goal which can be achieved within a measurable space of time. According to Etzioni (1968, p. 403) mobilization often begins with a project and it is easy to see why. Not only does it embody a common goal, the attainment of which is to the advantage of all, but it exemplifies that such goals really exist. It can be carried out within a limited period of time and thus postpones the difficult question of 'what is our ultimate goal?'. In addition, the project puts only a temporary demand upon the resources of those mobilized. As a socializing process, however, the project may lead to the peasants placing part of their resources permanently at the organization's disposal when they see that they are not being duped by some crafty leader. In farming communities such a project may be one that does not immediately lead to a conflict of interests with the landed proprietor, for example the building of schools and other community amenities. All three of the peasant organizations studied by Alberti (1970) began in this manner, and the same is true of the celebrated first Liga Camponesa in Brazil. Yet even newly formed conflict organizations not infrequently begin with a project. They aim at a concrete goal and attempt to achieve it; the enforcement of a particular law, the abolition of a hated obligation, a higher wage, shorter working hours.

The most important factor in overcoming cultural obstacles, however, is the presence of a *leader* with outstanding qualities, both instrumental and human. Huizer (1970, p. 192 f.) and also Lamond Tullis (1970, p. 225) speak of a charismatic leader. Why is such a leader with exceptional qualities necessary? In order to consider how peasants might improve their situation, it is first of all essential to possess more insight into this situation, its causes and component, interdependent elements than is usual among peasants. The patronage relationship, for instance, must be seen for what it is. At the same time it is necessary to draw up concrete aims which are, in theory, attainable, and to supervise the action this entails; the project must be planned. In addition it is essential that the action should be well organized, that no objectives be set and no actions undertaken which far exceed the capabilities of the peasants. To know exactly what one wishes to aim at implies a fairly considerable ability to evaluate the situation and the possibilities, including the possibilities of success and defeat at higher levels of decision. In the light of this we not surprisingly found that leaders often possess more non-agrarian experience, and more education, than their followers.

The personal qualities of the leaders are also of the utmost importance. In many cases (in our terms: in situation C and in situation A surrounded by large estates) the peasant community is often riddled with suspicion and envy. The only strong relationships are those with members of the family and a few privileged others, either friends or compadres. These latter relationships are, moreover, dyadic: they always involve two persons and no more. In such circumstances norms exist at most for traditional forms of co-operation – organizing festivities, helping each other on the land – but not for behaviour within an organization with a particular objective. In other cases, on large farms for instance, where there is much coming and going, one can scarcely speak of a community but more of a collection of individual families loosely related on the basis of varying criteria. In communities of this sort, the personality of the leader must be such that he gains the confidence of the majority of the peasants. He must in fact be someone with whom they would be willing to enter upon a dyadic relationship. Until the first success has been gained – and the economic motive for joining the organization becomes realistic – the leader must inspire sufficient confidence to unite the peasants and keep them united. He must not be corrupt and he must be able to convince the members of his good faith (for, apart from reprisals, the landed proprietors also attempt to neutralize the influence of the peasant leaders by bribing them, with promotion, an extra piece of land or something similar. Sometimes, it must be admitted, they are successful). He must, of course, possess authority; people must be prepared to do for the organization what he asks, not because they are complying with some norm or other regulating the behaviour of an organization member, for this norm frequently does not yet exist, but because it is he who asks. There is, however, a norm which governs acceptable behaviour towards one's partner in a dyadic relationship[13]. This, for the rest, implies that it is difficult for such a leader to extricate himself later; he has become accustomed to being the centre of things.

All we have said thus far proves that leaders are of crucial importance for the embryo organization. The more so when we recollect the importance, mentioned earlier, of contacts with possible allies on the national level. To a large extent, these will be *his* contacts.

3.7 Class awareness and the aims of mobilization

In concluding our attempt at a theory of mobilization, we must devote some words to the dawning awareness, among the peasants, of their common interests, to their class consciousness and to the objectives which they hope to achieve.

We have already pointed out that the various categories of peasants share the same interests only to a certain extent. This is all the more true since they tend to think in terms of the concrete, local situation as it affects them. At the same time we have observed that the presence of a local opponent helps to make them aware that they have interests in common.

We shall have occasion, in a later chapter dealing with solidarity – in other words, with the permanent allocation of individual resources in favour of the peasant organizations – to delve somewhat more deeply into the concept of *class*. The term is used in various meanings but we are usually referring to the collectivity of those who have no power, no possessions, a low income and few possibilities of development. It seems to me that this concept when applied to peasants, will describe a reality which for them exists only on the local level, and this for the reasons we have already given. Their means of production are of a local-territorial nature and their economic incorporation into a larger system is still far from complete. This also holds good for very many farms which sell most of their produce on the market and where the owner is in fact completely incorporated into the larger system. On the basis of the exploitation of the small – Indian – peasant, Frank (1967, ch. II) assumed that, contrary to what some earlier observers had asserted, they were indeed integrated into a larger economic system. This may very well correspond with an ideal notion, held by the same people, whereby getting rid of exploitation also implies an abolition of integration, the return to a reasonably prosperous isolated farming community, one not bound up in a long chain of inter-dependencies[14]. Peasants are often very much aware of the conflict of interests which arises between agriculturalists and urban consumers concerning the price of farm products. This makes them take a sceptical view of exhortations which would seem to suggest that they and the industrial proletariat form one class.

The terms in which the majority of peasants view the solution to their problems – a redistribution of land to individual farmers and government support for agriculture – are undeniably not class terms, but those of a local group. They do not aim to solve the problems of poverty as such, nor even of most of the poor. At best they are interested in the local poor. It is precisely this which lends that solution a slight air of unreality at the present time, certainly if the authorities engaged in pressing through the land reforms are preoccupied with the fate of all the poor. Such an administration can hardly permit itself to leave a large section of the poor peasants and agricultural workers out in the cold. Hobsbawm (1971, p. 11) has pointed out that the peasants' class programmes and slogans stand little chance of being put into practice, a fact which I myself had noted also (Galjart, 1971b).

This leaves two possibilities: either the peasants are mobilized for a programme which will not greatly appeal to them in the first instance, a programme in which the collectivization of agriculture occupies a prominent place, or they are mobilized for a much vaguer programme with which they can identify, a programme which promises land 'to those who till it' but does not specify how it will be distributed. Mobilization is more easily accomplished in the second case, although it seems possible for opponents to sow uncertainty among the peasants regarding the concrete outcome of a land reform, quoting examples derived from other societies.

Inherent in the second case, however, is the possibility that, once the land reforms have been carried out, the peasants may be gripped by disappointment and suspicion. In such cases the majority may then turn their backs again on the regime which introduced collectivization.

Our conclusion must be tragic. Unless the peasants mobilize, a more equitable distribution of land, income and power seems unlikely to materialize. Yet most of the small producers, and a large section of the agricultural workers, mobilize for the sake of an ideal – a piece of land they can call their own – which seems likely, under present circumstances, to remain only an ideal.

Notes

1 Not all the authors on this subject have made the attempt; the term campesino which is so handily rendered by peasant and suggests that we are dealing with one and the same category of the agrarian active population (i.e. those who earn their living through agriculture) may take the blame for this. Powell (1970) and Huizer (1970), for instance, speak of peasants tout court; the latter does not even define the term peasants.
2 It may be that a local élite monopolizes not so much the land as other desirable resources such as access to the market or to the government institutions. Such a monopoly may also lead to cultural patterns among the peasants such as those set out in the model.
3 In the literature dealing with the cultures of Indian farming communities – not infrequently to be found in situation C – mention is often made of levelling mechanisms. In a survey – which

for the rest does not state clearly to which of the situations we have distinguished here it refers – Erasmus (1968, p. 67) mentions terms like 'jealousy pattern', 'institutionalized envy' and 'invidious sanction' used by researchers to describe their results.

4 It was in order to draw attention to this that Queiroz (1963) called the small owners and squatters a forgotten category.

5 One of the most striking examples of this is the telegram reproduced in Vilaça and Cavalcanti (1965) and dated October 6th 1942. It was sent to a local police chief and landed proprietor in the state of Pernambuco, Brazil and read: 'We request you to reserve all the votes of Bom Conselho for Barros Barreto. Sincerely.'

6 This is not yet so in many countries with the result that half of the agrarian population does not vote and is thus uninteresting for the existing parties.

7 The argument in favour of such a request has become a standard formula: 'communist agitators coming from outside the area and who have no connection with agriculture, . . .'

8 A small, leftist, militant grouping is often unable to fulfil either function, since – cf. Anderson – it menaces the other power contenders to such an extent that it is not allowed to participate in decision making. I imagine that this is why such groups, even after initial successes, often do not find any permanent support among the peasants (cf. Galjart, 1969).

9 It is not surprising that in particular the internal relationships in rural areas have led to sociological theories in terms of dichotomous, conflicting classes. Examples of this are the theoretical concepts such as colonialismo interno, advanced by Gonzales Casanova, and (exploiting) metropolis and (exploited) periphery thought up by Frank. Although these theories, as Nickel (1971) attempts to show, are too loose to cover the entire reality, and suffer from the use of concepts which cannot be operationalized, at least they have the merit that no one, who studies development from a sociological point of view, can afford to ignore the problems they evoke.

10 The factors mentioned here also occur in Lamond Tullis' (1970) study of Peru. Unfortunately I did not manage to get hold of it until after I had written this chapter.

Tullis imitates Young (1966) in working with three concepts which he calls Capacity, Opportunity and Solidarity. Capacity is the measure in which a community is aware of new possibilities of behaviour in order to realize its own goals. Opportunity is the objective possibility possessed by this community of putting this new knowledge into practice. Solidarity is the measure in which the community possesses one value pattern and desires to realize it. Tullis postulates that as capacity grows, while opportunity grows more slowly or not at all, solidarity – which may then assume the form of a movement – increases. He calls the discrepancy between capacity and opportunity 'structural bind'.

In my terms: as familiarity with other alternatives increases (through the introduction of modern agricultural methods, education, travel, experiences in the city, proximity of the city) capacity grows. Opportunity increases with the decline of the power of the large landowners on a national level, and because peasants find allies on that level. However, the local attempt to preserve the status quo means that opportunity does not keep pace with capacity. In the resultant state of structural bind a movement of solidarity will emerge. Tullis too recognizes the need for charismatic leadership.

The terms in which Tullis couches his theory are at the same time more general and more vague than mine. The fact that they are more general is an advantage. The presence of a local opponent is indeed a very important example of what Tullis calls a structural bind, but it is not the only one. Adverse local conditions may also cause a structural bind and, correspondingly an attempt on the part of the community to surmount it.

11 In imitation of Hobsbawm this social banditry is indeed regarded as the first, albeit more or less individual, sign of protest; Quijano (1967) views it as the precursor of the later peasant movements. In order to prevent the romanticizing of the bandit it is well to remember what Blok (1967) has pointed out in a soberly written article; he stresses that in the long run the bandit also finds his victims among the poor agrarian population in which he causes internal divisions. Blok bases his criticism upon European data but he might just as easily have utilized the history of the celebrated Brazilian bandit, Lampião.

12 Earlier attempts in this direction have been made by researchers into the national character;

Moog, for instance, for Brazil (1954), Salazar Bondy for Peru (1969). The culture of poverty conceived by Lewis who worked principally in Mexico also deserves a mention in this context.

13 This view bears a relationship to what has been found elsewhere (Scheidlinger, 1958, p. 59), namely that 'in groups with an autocratic kind of leadership, the leader tends to replace the individual's superego. He assumes the role of a new inner authority and the tie to him is the basic cohesive force'.

14 Compare the interesting study of Mitrany (1961) which shows that the peasant movements and political parties, which flourished in Eastern Europe in the period between the two world wars, were in fact guided by similar ideals.

Chapter 4 Mobilization in Chile: testing part of the theory

4.1 Introduction

The theory presented in the preceding chapter was based upon conclusions arrived at by myself and other researchers and derived from data which was more often than not qualitative and collected anthropologically. In this chapter I shall attempt to test a number of hypotheses for Chile on the basis of quantitative data. As indicator for mobilization I chose the *degree of organization of agricultural workers in peasant syndicates*. This is calculated for each community by expressing the number of those organized[1] in the three large confederations of syndicates, El Triunfo Campesino, Ranquil and Libertad, as a percentage of the total agricultural wage labour force mentioned in the most recent agricultural census, that of March 1965. The following categories were included under wage labour: supervisory personnel, share cropper-inquilinos and inquilinos, permanent workers and the two categories of temporary labourers distinguished by the census. Out of the data found in the agricultural census indicators could be constructed for a part only of the variables and factors which were assumed in the previous chapter to influence the emergence and growth of peasant movements. In some cases the validity or reliability of an indicator is doubtful.

As the census unit was the municipality (comuna), we will be dealing exclusively with indicators for those independent variables which, we postulated, were important on the local level. Thus we have three indicators for the degree of agricultural development (the presence of irrigation, the use of artificial fertilizer, and the number of hectares per tractor); one indicator for owner absenteeism and consequent weakening of the patronage relationship (the occurrence of administrators), one indicator for the proximity of a large city (common boundaries with that city), a number of indicators for the presence of large agricultural enterprises in the comuna, one indicator for the degree of urbanization and and a number of indicators for the relative weight of the various status categories of farmers and workers and thus, perhaps, for the consequences of differences in status. All these indicators were calculated per comuna, usually in the form of percentages[2]. Other variables not mentioned in the previous chapter were also calculated. These concern principally the distribution of land, the significance of particular crops, the occurrence of property (in contrast to other forms of tenure) and the occurrence of land reform in the comuna up to August 1970[3].

4.2 Analysis of the differences between comunas with and without syndicates

Not only were the correlation coefficients between the degree of organization and the characteristics mentioned calculated, but also the average value of the characteristics in different categories of comuna. The average values showing degree of organization are given in Table 3.

At first sight the table seems to show that the degree of organization in comunas located near one of the three large cities i.e. Santiago, Valparaiso and Concepción is no higher than that in the remaining, more rural comunas. There seem to be two reasons for this surprising fact. In the first place it appears that a relatively larger number of those

Table 3. Average percentage organized wage labourers and average percentage members of the confederations El Triunfo Campesino, Ranquil and Libertad against the total of those organized, per comuna

Chile: 264 comunas	
% organized of total wage labour in agriculture	29
% members of El Triunfo of total organized	44
% members of Ranquil of total organized	22
% members of Libertad of total organized	13
Comunas possessing an agricultural workers' syndicate: 212 comunas	
% organized of total wage labour in agriculture	37
% members of El Triunfo of total organized	54
% members of Ranquil of total organized	27
% members of Libertad of total organized	16
Comunas situated close to one of the three large cities: 30 comunas[1]	
% organized of total wage labour in agriculture	28
% members of El Triunfo of total organized	18
% members Ranquil of total organized	29
% members Libertad of total organized	13
Remaining rural comunas: 234 comunas	
% organized of total wage labour in agriculture	29
% members El Triunfo of total organized	47
% members Ranquil of total organized	21
% members Libertad of total organized	13
Comunas where 50% or more of the population lives on the farms: 121 comunas	
% organized of total wage labour in agriculture	28
% members of El Triunfo of total organized	45
% members Ranquil of total organized	21
% members Libertad of total organized	11

1 Santiago, Valparaiso and Concepcion were regarded as large cities. Comunas situated close to these cities are characterized by having a common boundary with one of them.

Table 4. Geographical position of comunas with and without agricultural workers' syndicates

	Close to large city	Not close to large city
Syndicate	19	193
No syndicate	11	41

comunas located close to the cities, do not possess a syndicate at all. This is shown in Table 4. If we leave aside for the moment the 52 comunas without a syndicate, it appears that the degree of organization is indeed higher in the comunas located near the large cities than elsewhere, namely 44 % as against 36 %. Although we must return to the question of why relatively more comunas without syndicates occur close to cities, the hypothesis that the degree of organization is higher closer to the cities does seem to be correct.

The second reason why this hypothesis is not immediately confirmed by Table 3 is the deviant behaviour of the confederation El Triunfo Campesino. This confederation consisted largely of syndicates set up by INDAP during the Frei government (INDAP was one of the two government bodies involved with agrarian reform). El Triunfo appears to be more important in the rural areas than close to the large cities. Mobilization under government guidance turned out differently therefore from the mobilization led by non-official persons or groups – INDAP evidently paid particular attention to comunas as yet unorganized, those far from the cities and where agriculture was less developed. El Triunfo, as it were, filled in the blank spaces on the map. This is obvious from the following fact, as well as from the averages in Table 3. If we examine the 212 comunas in which syndicates occur, the percentage of those organized who are members of El Triunfo – in contrast to the picture presented by Ranquil and Libertad – appears to correlate negatively $(R = -0.28)$ with the overall degree of organization. In other words, the more organized workers in a comuna who belong to El Triunfo, the lower the total percentage of organized wage labourers. El Triunfo is chiefly important in places where there is little organization. El Triunfo also occurs more frequently as the sole organization in a comuna. This happens 74 times, whereas it occurs with a Ranquil syndicate only in 24 comunas and with a Libertad syndicate only in 11.

The deviant behaviour of El Triunfo clearly demonstrates the importance of the government role in peasant mobilization and organization. Everywhere throughout the country INDAP had small so-called area-offices each provided with a number of promoters whose only task was to help organize the agricultural workers on the estates. These people evidently took the opportunity of setting up syndicates in places where these could not automatically be expected according to the hypotheses mentioned in the previous chapter. Does this now mean that these hypotheses are related more to promoters who have to come out from a town and are often dependent upon public transport than to the actual situation of the peasants? Probably not entirely so. INDAP was a government body and each of its offices was linked by telephone with the provincial and national head offices. It was easier for El Triunfo to mobilize allies than it was for the other two confederations. Moreover it will appear that, despite the deviant behaviour of El Triunfo, i.e. the government influence upon the process, many of the hypotheses were nonetheless confirmed.

Table 5 provides us with more information concerning the differences between those comunas which have a syndicate and those which do not. The first that meets the eye is the importance of the proximity of a large city. The confederations Ranquil and Libertad, but particularly Ranquil, have their most important bases close to the aforementioned three large cities. However, the proximity of a large city appears also to specify the relationship between degree of organization and certain characteristics of the agrarian structure. For example, in the countryside, the comuna without a syndicate is

Table 5. Averages of characteristics of the agrarian structure for organized and non-organized comunas

Variable	All Chilean comunas		Comunas near the 3 large cities		Comunas not near a city	
	without org. (N = 52)	with org. (N = 212)	without org. (N = 11)	with org. (N = 19)	without org. (N = 41)	with org. (N = 193)
(1) Organized in syndicates of wage labour[1] (%)	0	37	0	45	0	36
(2) Members of El Triunfo of total organized (%)	0	54	0	29	0	57
(3) Members of Ranquil of total organized (%)	0	27	0	46	0	25
(4) Members of Libertad of total organized (%)	0	16	0	21	0	16
(9) Producers and unpaid relatives of working population[2] (%)	73	54	57	43	77	54
(10) Sharecroppers-inquilinos and inquilinos of working population (%)	4	10	10	12	3	10
(11) Sharecroppers-inquilinos and inquilinos of wage labour (%)	16	23	26	21	14	23
(12) Permanent labourers of working population (%)	7	14	15	22	5	13
(13) Permanent labourers of wage labour (%)	28	31	32	43	26	29
(14) Temporary labourers of working population (%)	11	19	12	17	11	19
(15) Temporary labourers of wage labour (%)	48	41	26	29	54	42
(18) Farms 0–2 ha of total farms (%)	18	36	41	61	12	34
(19) Farms 2–10 ha of total farms (%)	28	27	32	21	27	28
(25) Farms ⩾ 1000 ha of total farms ⩾ 200 ha (%)	26	32	37	25	23	32
(26) Land of farms under administrator of total farmland (%)	31	48	54	54	25	48
(27) Privately owned farms of total farms (%)	56	42	54	41	56	42
(28) Irrigated land of total area cultivable land (%)	19	40	51	71	10	37
(29) Farming population of total comuna population (%)	48	46	13	22	57	49
(31) Artificially fertilized land of total cultivable land (%)	12	27	27	39	8	26
(42) Number of hectares cultivable land per tractor	387	217	72	15	470	238

1 In this and the following tables we understand by wage labour the total of male wage workers in agriculture above 15 years of age.
2 In this and the following tables we understand by working population the total male working population in agriculture above 15 years of age.

the most rural (i.e. the percentage of population living on farms is higher there); close to the large cities, however, the non-organized comuna is the least rural in this respect. Another example: in the rural areas it is precisely in the organized comunas that relatively more large farms are found; close to the city the opposite seems to be the case. Table 6 shows that for all sizes of farming the sign of the relationship between their occurrence and the degree of organization differs in the countryside from that in the comunas located near a large city. To give one more example: in the countryside the presence of an administrator (which serves here as an indicator of owner absenteeism, a factor assumed to contribute to the weakening of patronage relationships) is, as we expected, more frequent in the syndicalized comunas; close to the city this factor seems unimportant.

Other variables appear to play a role both in the rural areas and in the comunas close to the large cities. In both cases the organized comuna seems to have a more developed form of agriculture with more irrigation, more artificial fertilizer and more tractors. The difference, however, is more pronounced in the rural areas.

Both close to the cities and in the more rural areas the organized comunas number, on average, more permanent workers among the active agrarian population. Together with the inquilinos and the sharecroppers it is they among the wage workers who join syndicates. The occurrence of temporary labourers among the wage workers correlates fairly negatively with the degree of organization, but in Table 5 this is only evident from the averages in the rural areas. Close to the big cities there is yet another difference between organized and non-organized comunas which is not immediately apparent from the figures. The only category which was included among the wage workers but for which no separate percentages were calculated is that of supervisory personnel. Whereas in the rural areas and in the organized comunas close to the city this category accounts for between 5 and 6% of the wage-earners, it appears to reach about 16% in the non-organized comunas close to the big cities. The relatively high significance of this category, which is generally not affiliated to any syndicate, is better paid than the ordinary workers and often regards promotion as a favour granted by the patron on the basis of a good personal relationship, helps in my view to explain the absence of a syndicate in these comunas.

What picture now emerges of the non-organized comunas close to one of the three large cities? One of a comuna with a small agricultural population, working for the greater part on family farms; a smaller section works on the relatively frequent large enterprises which are chiefly devoted to extensive cattle raising. The principal reason why the inquilinos and permanent wage workers are not organized is probably their physical isolation; small numbers on large cattle-raising estates. A possible supplementary reason is that they include a fairly large number of supervisors who are generally not attracted to syndicates. Finally INDAP evidently took less trouble to organize the wage earners in the vicinity of the large cities; there El Triunfo is less important than Ranquil.

In the rural areas we obtain a similar picture of the non-organized comunas. Admittedly the agrarian working population there is large, but the majority work on family farms. Among the wage workers the important category is that of the temporary labourers, who are difficult to organize (and who possibly originate from the small, inadequate minifundia). Agriculture is backward, a factor which apparently accompanies physical isolation; the roads are bad. Many owners of large farming enterprises (who are the most inclined to appoint administrators to do their work) live on their ranches. This probably encourages both patronage and oppression; they oppose syndicalization.

In general these pictures confirm the hypotheses mentioned in the previous chapter. We find for instance the influence of the following factors confirmed:

– the development of agriculture;
– the proximity of urban centres;
– the difference between various categories of the agrarian population, depending upon their place in the production process; notably the difference between permanent and temporary agricultural workers;
– owner absenteeism;
– the crucial role of the government.

There proved to be one other important factor. It is partially implied in the first two mentioned but we ourselves have not referred to it before. The physical isolation of the peasants may explain why some places have a syndicate while others do not.

48

4.3 Correlations of the degree of organization

For Chile as a whole the comparison between averages of different categories of comuna, applied above, appeared more fruitful than the analysis of correlation coefficients between the degree of organization and the other variables. Table 6 contains a number of coefficients for various categories of Chilean comunas.

The table shows that, for Chile as a whole as well as for the typically rural comunas, the degree of organization correlates with the relative significance of the various categories of the agrarian population. The more sharecropper-inquilinos, inquilinos and permanent labourers among the wage workers, the higher the degree of organization. This lessens as the percentage of temporary workers increases. Thus the temporary workers are indeed less inclined towards affiliation, or more difficult to organize, than those who have a permanent job on the farms. The percentage of extremely large farms (larger than 1000 ha) compared with all farms larger than 200 ha also correlates to some extent with the degree of organization.

We have already encountered one reason for the scanty nature of the correlation coefficients. Some of the variables interweave and so conceal each other. Moreover, the

Table 6. Correlation coefficients (Pearson r) between degree of organization and a number of characteristics of the agrarian structure, per comuna

Variable	Chile (N = 264)	Comunas close to large city (N = 30)	Remaining comunas (N = 234)	Typical rural comunas (N = 121)
(9) Producers and unpaid members of working population	−0.12	0.04	−0.15	−0.29
(10) Sharecroppers-inquilinos and inquilinos of working population	0.19	−0.01	0.24	0.45
(11) Sharecroppers-inquilinos and inquilinos of wage labour	0.27	−0.11	0.35	0.44
(12) Permanent labourers of working population	0.22	0.39	0.21	0.30
(13) Permanent labourers of wage labour	0.24	0.64	0.16	0.22
(14) Temporary labourers of working population	−0.09	−0.32	−0.07	−0.02
(15) Temporary labourers of wage labour	−0.36	−0.45	−0.37	−0.49
(18) Farms 0–2 ha of total farms	0.14	0.14	0.15	0.38
(19) Farms 2–10 ha of total farms	0.03	−0.48	0.11	0.03
(20) Farms 10–50 ha of total farms	−0.12	0.13	−0.16	−0.29
(21) Farms 50–200 ha of total farms	−0.04	0.42	−0.12	−0.21
(22) Farms 200–500 ha of total farms	−0.05	0.28	−0.11	−0.25
(23) Farms ⩾500 ha of total farms	0.01	−0.04	0.02	−0.06
(24) Farms 200–500 ha of farms ⩾200 ha	−0.07	0.10	−0.11	−0.10
(25) Farms ⩾ 1000 ha of farms ⩾200 ha	0.19	−0.11	0.24	0.33
(26) Land of farms with administrator of all farm land	0.14	−0.20	0.22	0.38
(27) Privately owned farms of total number of farms	−0.15	−0.03	−0.17	−0.20
(28) Irrigated surface of total area cultivable land	0.02	−0.26	0.07	0.23
(29) Farming population of total in the comuna	−0.08	0.14	−0.14	−0.25
(31) Land treated with artificial fertilizer of total cultivable land	0.06	−0.12	0.12	0.34
(42) Number of hectares cultivable land per tractor	−0.11	−0.09	−0.14	−0.28

influence of certain variables may not be linear but curvilinear. Let us take for example the degree of agricultural development. We earlier found confirmation of our hypothesis that organization occurs wherever agriculture is more developed. We also discovered, however, that this relation did not hold good under all circumstances. From an agricultural viewpoint the unorganized comunas close to the three large cities were more advanced than the organized comunas in the more rural areas. Something similar occurs with regard to the presence of administrators (indicator for owner absenteeism). It was our hypothesis that the more administrators there were, the greater the chance of a syndicate. This hypothesis was confirmed for those comunas some distance away from the city, but it also appeared that in the non-organized comunas close to a city the percentage of administrators is greater than in the organized comunas in the rural areas.

Since the proximity of a city and the degree of urbanization of the various comunas seems to play such an important role that it obscures the link between other variables and the occurrence of a syndicate, we have set out separately in Table 6 the correlation coefficients between degree of organization and the remaining variables for the typically rural comunas. For these comunas the correlations with indicators for the development of agriculture, (nos. 28, 31, 42), for economic development (no. 29) and for owner absenteeism (no. 26) appear notably stronger than for Chile as a whole and in the direction we had suggested. For the categories of working population and wage labour the correlations we discovered earlier are confirmed. The more family farms (and people working on them: nos. 9, 20, 21) the less organized the wage-workers. The more sharecroppers, inquilinos and permanent workers among the agrarian population, the more likely they are to be organized in syndicates. The more large farms (no. 25) the higher the degree of organization. Here too the presence of temporary labourers within the category of wage workers proves to correlate extremely negatively with the degree of organization. Our hypotheses are thus confirmed for the typically rural comunas.

4.4 Multiple regression analysis to explain the degree of organization

In order to gain more insight into the way in which the variables are connected, we have carried out both a multiple and a partial correlation analysis. The results for the three categories of comunas which preoccupied us earlier are gathered together in Table 7. The analysis tabulates the independent variables according to the size of their partial correlation coefficient with the dependent variable. This means that the other independent variables are kept constant. This partial correlation coefficient is mentioned separately. The column 'Fraction explained' indicates the *direct* contribution of the variable in question to explaining the variance of the dependent variable, in our case the degree of organization. In column R^2 one should only pay attention to the bottom line which indicates what percentage of the variance in the degree of organization is explained by the independent variables taken together. It is impossible to assess immediately from the column 'Fraction explained' the importance of the total contribution of a variable. A variable may contribute little directly but a great deal indirectly. Nor is it true simply to say that if variables (A and B for instance) are omitted by the programme because their partial correlation coefficient with the dependent variable is very small, then the hypothesis which postulated that they were important for the degree of organization is entirely incorrect. They may correlate strongly with another variable which has been

Table 7. Results of multiple and partial correlation calculations to explain the degree of organization in different categories of comuna. R^2 is cumulating squared multiple correlation coefficient

Variable	R^2	Partial correlation coefficient	Fraction explained
Comunas close to one of the 3 large cities (N = 30)			
(13) Permanent labourers of wage labour	0.40	0.73	0.35
(31) Artificially fertilized land of total cultivable land	0.42	−0.49	0.09
(25) Farms ≥1000 ha of total farms ≥200 ha	0.44	−0.45	0.08
(19) Farms 2–10 ha of total farms	0.55	−0.51	0.11
(29) Farming population of total comuna population	0.61	0.31	0.03
(26) Land under administrators of total farm land	0.69	0.46	0.08
Comunas not close to one of the 3 large cities (N = 234)			
(11) Sharecroppers-inquilinos of wage labour	0.12	0.40	0.14
(13) Permanent labourers of wage labour	0.18	0.27	0.06
(19) Farms 2–10 ha of total farms	0.19	0.16	0.02
(9) Producers and unpaid relatives of working population	0.25	−0.21	0.03
(25) Farms ≥1000 ha of total farms ≥200 ha	0.257	0.10	0.01
Typical rural comunas (N = 121)			
(15) Temporary labourers of wage labour	0.23	−0.39	0.10
(25) Farms ≥1000 ha of total farms ≥200 ha	0.27	0.19	0.02
(18) Farms 0–2 ha of total farms	0.36	0.19	0.02
(29) Farming population of total comuna population	0.38	−0.21	0.03
(28) Irrigated surface of total cultivable land	0.39	0.16	0.02
(31) Artificially fertilized land of total cultivable land	0.40	0.15	0.01
(22) Farms 200–500 ha of total farms	0.44	−0.24	0.04

retained (for instance Z) and so provide no distinctive contribution. Had Z not been included in the analysis, then A and B would occur among the variables retained. All this means that our lack of insight into the reasons for the link between the variables which define the agrarian structure may mislead us. It is possible that there not only seems to be, but must be, a link between let us say, irrigation, the occurrence of large farms, the relative preponderance of a particular category of the rural labour force and the presence of administrators. However, we have no theory to explain this, so that it is sometimes impossible to say why one variable is retained and another not.

The table shows that in the three categories of comunas different percentages of the variance in the degree of organization are explained, namely, 69%, 26%, and 44%. This is not necessarily because in the countryside, unlike those areas close to the cities, other variables, not included in our research, have a role to play. A simpler explanation would be that the more comunas involved in our calculation, the greater the number of divergent findings and measurement errors. This is indeed so. It also appears that almost all the irregular, unexpected, percentages of the degree of organization concern deviations upwards. A lower degree of organization would be expected on the basis of the regression coefficients.

In those comunas situated close to cities the following variables seem to contribute to explain the variance in the degree of mobilization: the relative significance of permanent wage workers, owner absenteeism and the rural character. A negative contribution is provided by agricultural development, the presence of very large farms and of very small ones (probably horticultural). The more there are of these the less the degree of syndical organization.

Less easy to interpret, however, are the negative signs for the partial coefficients of artificial fertilizer use and large farms. They may indicate either the presence of intensive horticulture or of intensive cattle breeding.

In the other comunas an important factor is, once again, the relative preponderance of share-croppers, inquilinos and permanent workers in the totality of wage labour (and, negatively, the presence of independent peasants employing members of their own family). The occurrence of farms of between 2 and 10 hectares also plays a role, but one opposite to that in the 'urban' comunas. This time the relation with the degree of organization is positive.

In the typically agrarian communities the relative significance of the temporary wage workers appears to be of great importance, as does both the occurrence of very large farms (>1000 ha) and of very small ones (0–2 ha). Together, these variables may indicate the presence of the so-called latifundia—minifundia complex. The degree of urbanization also contributes as does the stage of agricultural development indicated by the use of artificial fertilizer.

It must be pointed out that the variable making the most important direct contribution in the interpretation, the occurrence of temporary workers, must not simply be interpreted as meaning that the temporary workers did not *wish* to organize. It may well be that the syndicates, which were legally restricted in their operations to a single comuna, were thereby rendered unattractive to this category of worker. Although we run the risk of making a category-mistake, this interpretation is in line with that of various other authors.

Despite the fact that only one variable was retained in all three of the calculations the data nonetheless show that the composition of the agrarian working population, the occurrence of really large farms, the degree of urbanization and the measure of agricultural development (indicated by the use of artificial fertilizer) provide the most important clues in explaining the variance in the degree of organization. They explain between 30% and 70%.

We can leave aside the variables with regard to the composition of the labour force and the farm size distribution in order to see more clearly the role played by the remaining variables. These relate to the significance of:

the occurrence of very large farms   (Variable 25)
the occurrence of administrators   (Variable 26)
the occurrence of irrigation   (Variable 28)
the rural nature of the comunas   (Variable 29)
the significance of permanent crops   (Variable 30)
the occurrence of tractors   (Variable 31)
productivity per hectare compared with the rest of the province   (Variable 32)

Using only these variables a multiple correlation analysis was done for different categories of comunas with the degree of organization as the variable to be explained.

Table 8. Results of multiple and partial correlation calculations with selected independent variables to explain the degree of organization of different categories of comuna. R^2 is cumulating squared multiple correlation coefficient

Variable	R^2	Fraction explained	Partial regression coefficient
All comunas (N = 264)			
(25) the occurrence of very large farms	0.03	0.04	0.21
(31) the occurrence of tractors	0.04	0.01	0.12
(28) the occurrence of irrigation	0.05	0.01	−0.10
All comunas (N = 256)[1]			
(25) The occurrence of very large farms	0.06	0.04	0.21
(31) The occurrence of tractors	0.09	0.02	0.15
(28) The occurrence of irrigation	0.10	0.01	−0.13
(26) The occurrence of administrators	0.11	0.01	0.12
(32) Productivity per ha compared with the rest of the province	0.13	0.01	0.11
Comunas near a city (N = 30)			
(28) The occurrence of irrigation	0.07	0.07	−0.27
Comunas not near a city (N = 234)			
(25) The occurrence of very large farms	0.06	0.05	0.23
(31) The occurrence of tractors	0.07	0.01	0.10
(29) The rural nature of the comunas	0.08	0.01	−0.11
Typical rural comunas (N = 121)			
(25) The occurrence of very large farms	0.10	0.12	0.37
(29) The rural nature of the comunas	0.20	0.06	−0.29
(31) The occurrence of tractors	0.27	0.07	0.30
Typical rural comunas (N = 118)[1]			
(25) The occurrence of very large farms	0.18	0.18	0.48
(31) The occurrence of tractors	0.35	0.14	0.42
(29) The rural nature of the comunas	0.38	0.03	−0.22

1 Excluded are those comunas, in which it appears that 100% or more of the wage labourers are organized; in other words those comunas in which some of the self-employed have most probably also become members of the syndicate.

The results are given in Table 8.

This table, which must be considered in conjunction with Table 7, reveals a number of facts. It appears that the variables relating to the composition of the working population and the distribution of property do indeed provide an important contribution of their own in explaining the variance in the degree of organization; the explained percentages in Table 8 are significantly lower. This does not mean, however, that the variables relating to the modernity of the agricultural methods have no role at all to play; they also contribute, albeit to a lesser degree.

It is also evident that the few strongly divergent observation results (i.e. comunas in which the wage labour appears 100% organized) detract sharply from the explanatory value of the variables. The elimination of only 8 divergent communities out of the 264 doubled the percentage of variance explained and also restored the explanatory role of a couple of the variables which had dropped out when the divergent results were retained. Even with the typically rural comunas the effect of removing only three divergent results was considerable.

With regard to the 30 comunas situated close to a city it must be observed that in the first instance the explanatory variables, taken together, explained 28 % of the variation. They were, however, successively eliminated as having a (too) low T-value. This proves that in these comunas there is a fairly capricious interplay of very many factors.

The explanatory variables function best in the typically rural comunas. Most important are the degree of urbanization, the occurrence of large farms and of tractors.

4.5 Conclusion

All in all the statistical processing of the material indicates strongly that the social-economic development of the comuna itself and of agriculture within the comuna, the extent of urbanization, the occurrence of very large farms and, occasionally, owner absenteeism, influence the degree of organization. Also, the workers for whom it makes sense to organize should not be merely a small minority of the agrarian population. Given the incomplete nature of the figures and indicators I am inclined to view the quantitative results as confirming at least part of the theory presented in the previous chapter.

The results also have an important bearing upon a very topical question. Does agricultural development hinder or promote a structural revolution in the rural areas of the developing countries? For Chile it would seem that development encouraged peasant mobilization. This, however, may also be partly attributed to the fact that the law governing syndicalization made it difficult for the temporary workers to organize. It is less easy for them to 'get tough' in the couple of months they spend working for an owner. Having conceded this much, however, I still believe that population pressure on the land and the emergence of a temporary agricultural proletarian work force are not sufficient to ensure mobilization. It would seem that this occurs only after a certain stage of development has been reached.

Notes

1 According to the data published in March 1970 by the Fondo de Educacion y Extension Sindical of the Ministry of Labour.
2 The comunas situated in the three most northerly provinces, as well as eight comunas belonging to the conglomeration Gran Santiago were not taken into consideration since agriculture is found there rarely or not at all. The most northern province for our purposes was, therefore, Coquimbo.
3 I am grateful to C. W. M. de Ranitz, H. van de Belt, P. Spijkers and Mineke de Regt for their patient and meticulous computation of the data.

Chapter 5 Mobilization with no local opponent: the small independent peasants and their co-operative

5.1 Introduction

In the model reproduced in Chapter 3, peasant communities were distinguished according to the local distribution of land. There are peasant communities in Latin America where the land is more or less equally divided (situation A) or where, although the allocation is unequal, the large majority of the population owns some land (situation B).

In such situations many of the peasants may well be poor, but there is mostly no question of a direct, local opponent. In other words their poverty does not simply result from another member of the community's directly appropriating whatever surplus they produce.

In such situations too it seems advisable to promote co-operation as soon as the desire for better living conditions begins to become general. In other words, the peasants seem ripe for mobilization towards the achievement of a shared goal, the improvement of their standard of living. The most suitable organization for this purpose is probably the co-operative, for the main interests of peasants in such situations are those of small but independent agrarian producers. The co-operative may serve two purposes: provide countervailing power on the market for agricultural products and confer advantages of scale in purchasing inputs or in utilizing machinery. This would in effect be mobilization on the basis of a particular interest, that of the producers, in order to achieve a particular form of collaboration, the co-operative.

It must be made clear from the start that modern forms of co-operation in the field of production cannot be introduced without a radical change of values on the part of the independent peasant producer. At the level of economic development attained by the communities under discussion here, the family is the most important productive and consumer unit, in short the most important social unit for the peasant. His whole life-style and methods of work are adapted to that unit. It is thus not surprising that, with this frame of reference, these values, he will tend to reject a production structure which does not start from the family as the principal social unit, but rather from the local peasant communty. I shall return to this problem later. I mention this in order to explain why the co-operatives to which these peasants belong are nearly always service co-operatives. We shall thus confine ourselves for the present to that form of mobilization aimed at setting up a service co-operative. Two cases will be distinguished, the spontaneous and the induced.

5.2 The spontaneous setting up of co-operatives

At the level of agricultural development where most of the peasants still produce mainly for their own consumption, selling only a surplus, co-operation is needed, but not a co-operative. In such circumstances traditional forms of co-operation may be found, such as mutual help when labour is short, or in building a house, or, occasionally, in times of sickness.

It would be mistaken to assume that the survival of such customs automatically implies that the peasants would welcome a co-operative, a formal new association. The need for a formal organization like a co-operative only makes itself felt at a higher level of agricultural development or among peasants who have already attained that higher level on their farms. The course of events in Chile illustrates this quite clearly. In 1970 this country possessed two kinds of agricultural co-operatives. One of these, the cooperativa agricola whose members consisted mainly of the larger farmers, those with, say, 40, 80 or 150 hectares of irrigated land, was usually founded by the farmers themselves and was economically prosperous. The government, however, had usually initiated the other kind, the cooperativa campesina, intended for the small farmers, and mostly in a very weak economic position. I came across another instance during my research in an agricultural settlement in Brazil. After two attempts by a state institution to set up a co-operative had failed, it was precisely the larger farmers and aspiring landowners who wished to venture a third attempt (Galjart, 1968, p. 105).

It is hardly surprising to find that the peasants who feel the need for a co-operative are those whose farms have attained a certain stage of development. They purchase more means of production, they produce greater quantities and thus have more to sell and more interest in good market outlets. They are beginning to use machines which could be bought by the co-operative and hired out to them. In short, they begin to feel the need for an institution which would be advantageous to them in buying, selling and in various stages of the production process. These more modern peasants are often those with the larger holdings. It may also be, of course, that the spontaneous setting up of a co-operative is induced after all by the advantages, fiscal and otherwise, promised to co-operatives by the government in order to promote the movement. Advantages of this sort are naturally more interesting for the larger peasant producers. In fact a co-operative may sometimes be nothing more than a concealed firm belonging to a handful of large producers.

If the large producers decide to set up a co-operative the (small) peasants in the district may join, but their membership will be to some extent marginal. Quantitatively or qualitatively, the co-operative provides them with fewer services. Since the organization supplies a recognized need, and most of the founders dispose of some capital, a spontaneous co-operative like this often succeeds in building up capital, expanding the services provided and realizing its aim of providing countervailing power and scale advantages.

5.3 The induced co-operative

The position is entirely different in those agrarian communities which are as yet comparatively undeveloped. As we have pointed out these will be familiar with other forms of co-operation, but there will usually be no need for a co-operative as such. However, this need *is* felt by the government, the planners, or other outsiders who would like to see the community develop. We shall deal later with the ideals and expectations, often implicit, which frequently motivate such outsiders. Suffice it to say that everywhere in the third world the co-operative is seized upon by governments and other developers as an institution which might contribute to agricultural development. In other words the local co-operative is usually founded by agencies or individuals who are themselves products of a system which embraces the community. At the very least they take the initiative and insistently urge the local population to set up such an association. In 'ideal-typical' terms this process of induced mobilization and association displays the following characteristics:

1. A government agency or an individual with local influence (such as the local priest), convinced of the great utility of a co-operative discusses the idea with local peasants and, once interest has been aroused, seeks local, informal leaders to call the peasants together and persuade them to set up a co-operative.

2. Although, comparing their standard of living with that of the urban middle classes, all peasants are poor, there are always local differences. One is poorer than the other and has less land. It will therefore be the larger, somewhat better off, more modern and more productive peasants who will show the most interest and be the first to join up.[1] These peasants too will usually be elected to the administrative positions. There are a number of explanations for the dominant role they soon begin to play in the induced co-operatives.

– They are better able to bear the initial sacrifice which membership entails.

– As we have already observed with regard to the spontaneous co-operatives, it is the somewhat larger peasant farmers who will benefit most from the services offered by the co-operative.

– A government inspired co-operative is usually accompanied by the extension of a certain amount of credit. The somewhat larger, more innovative peasant producers are better able to avail of this and are more willing and able to take the risks which inevitably accompany the application of new methods.

– In a later phase, once the co-operative has been started, the allocation of further credit is often particularistic in a country where funds are insufficient to extend credit to every poor peasant. It is thus very important for every co-operative to have established good relationships, or otherwise be able to influence this allocation to the advantage of its own members. This is where patronage rears its head, in the form of brokerage. It is precisely the larger peasants in the community who possess the largest number or the best channels of communication with the allocating government agencies. This fact – and the realization among the members that such channels are essential if credit is to be obtained – is reason enough for electing precisely these larger peasants to the committee of the co-operative.

– Another reason is that the larger peasants also maintain more local patronage relationships, have dispensed more favours and are better able to mobilize the members' votes.

– Such peasants often find posts in the committee for the simple reason that – as an after-effect of the principles of Rochdale and since the co-operative is usually poor – such work is not remunerated. Accordingly committee members must have time to spare, or to put it another way, have a sufficiently high income not to have to work all day and every day.

3. As we have already pointed out, the co-operative will often concentrate on those services which are of most interest to the somewhat larger peasants. This is not only because they themselves, as members of the committee, will tend to identify their own problems with those of under-developed local agriculture in general. In fact the whole view of agricultural development underlying the setting up of such co-operatives is a technical one. The solution is sought in increased production and productivity. Generally speaking the co-operatives are in a bad position to fulfil one of the services eagerly desired by the smaller peasants, namely the provision of cheap consumer goods. Insufficient capital prevents them from supplying such goods on credit as the local shopkeeper is able to do. Any attempt to provide this service will probably result in financial disaster – assisted by the almost ever present inflation.

4. Those peasants who become members of an induced co-operative are, generally, too poor to provide their organization with a working capital of any great size. The co-operative thus remains dependent upon government credit, which as we have already mentioned is extended in a rather particularistic manner and for which patronage channels – and leaders possessing such channels – usually remain necessary.

5. Large loans are not infrequently granted on the basis of projects and plans into which too little research has been done. A crop is recommended and sown and does badly. A machine is bought and proves to cost far too much to run. A limiting factor which is almost always underestimated is the management capacity of the committee members or limited staff of the co-operative, or of the peasants themselves. After only a few years the book-keeping is in such a muddle that it is impossible to tell whether money is being embezzled or not. Naturally this provides much food for suspicion and scandal. The activities undertaken by the co-operative are often so badly managed and organized that it works at a loss instead of showing the expected profit. The paradoxical situation occurs that a person with sufficient qualities to run such an induced co-operative is expected to do so for a low salary whereas if he worked for himself he would probably be quite well off in a couple of years. (Two of my Chilean informants, officials of INDAP, whom I considered to be among the best, the most well-intentioned and the most capable of my Chilean acquaintances, confessed that when a few years ago the co-operatives they were assisting received large government loans 'we simply began to produce. We didn't worry about whether our projects would pay or not. We weren't even aware of the problem.' In 1970, however, it was only supplementary credit from the government which saved the communal poultry enterprises initiated by the peasants, although they continued to make a loss and failed even to recover their running costs). The results achieved by a co-operative or its members with the capital credit extended to them are crucial for the further course of events within the co-operative. If it succeeds in making a profit and in transforming credit into capital, then the co-operative acquires greater financial elbow room and has, moreover, discovered an activity capable of exploitation by the management quality at its disposal.

6. The phenomena mentioned under point 5 explain why, in so very many cases, the credit extended by the government is not earned back by the peasants and cannot, accordingly, be paid back. The government, which does not dispose of unlimited funds and which, in a democracy, is also convinced that there is more political advantage and prestige to be gained by embarking on a brand new project elsewhere rather than by laboriously rehabilitating one which may have been started by a previous government,

simply cuts off credit.

7. It is extremely likely that, once the supply of credit from the government dries up, the co-operative will, to all intents and purposes, cease to exist. The members who joined, not so much because they felt such a need for a co-operative but often in the anticipation of receiving considerable credit, begin to lose interest and to drift away. The suspicion and gossip, the mutual recriminations have, in the meantime, undermined relationships within the community. Committee members depart and are replaced by people less able. On passing through the district five years later, the observer can often detect no trace of the large amounts of credit dispensed, which must have been spent on something, let alone of the co-operative.

5.4 The implicit ideology

We have described, in ideal-typical terms, how a spontaneous and an induced co-operative respectively can originate and, sometimes, vanish again. We had the service co-operative in mind, not the production type, since the latter can only develop under completely different conditions. One might wonder why a government, planners or other experts in the field of agriculture undertake projects which so often seem destined to fail. The reason, it seems to me, is that these experts and the government in question cherish all kinds of notions and expectations which are, in fact, incorrect.

In the first place, the reality is often lost sight of that a co-operative only satisfies the peasants' needs after they have reached a certain stage of development. Yet a co-operative is induced at an earlier stage because it is expected to provide something which is really beyond its capabilities. It is expected to bring about a local economic development which will benefit *all* the peasants. But even if the co-operative is a roaring success from the economic point of view, the agricultural development to which it contributes will merely serve to increase the inequality between peasants. The better peasant farmers (which often means, unfortunately, the originally better-off farmers, those with a little more land, a trifle higher income, more education, more contacts with urban culture) outdistance their less successful colleagues in income, status and eventually, in the size of their holdings. Not only does the service co-operative not hamper this process, it even encourages it. Thus a government frequently expects of such co-operatives results which do not correspond at all with those actually achieved, that is, if the co-operative does not fail completely. In all probability governments continue to cling to these expectations because they accord with the preference, frequently cherished by western experts, for family farms. They also accord with the values held by the majority of the independent peasants in the developing country itself. In addition, they help gloss over the problem of the productive organization. The expectations thus add up to an ideology, but are in fact incorrect. The only form of co-operative which prevents the growth of social and economic inequality in agricultural development, and then only within each group, is the production co-operative. It will be clear that the inducing of such co-operatives must be based upon a political decision taken at national level. It also implies that the peasants must be convinced that this is their only way of achieving a higher standard of living. The setting up of a co-operative must therefore be preceded or accompanied by a radical indoctrination process. It is often found that even in situation A, where levelling mechanisms exist and are accepted, this does not automatically imply the acceptance of equality as a value in a new production organization, or the acceptance of a new levelling mechanism. In this respect there is no room for any of the naïveté such as that displayed by, for instance, Fals Borda in his introduction to the studies on Latin-American Co-operatives by Pugh *et al.* (1970).

Some people (Stavenhagen, 1966 for instance) state that co-operative agricultural enterprises cannot even survive in an economy where other sectors consist of individually owned enterprises. I think that they can, provided that the co-operative farm helps to achieve another, justified value of the peasants', namely a higher standard of living, and does so more efficiently than would a farm of their own. This at least was one of the conclusions I arrived at during my research in Chile. Those of my Chilean colleagues who were primarily interested in the social consequences of the new peasant organizations that aimed at co-operative production, and who considered the economic consequences to be of lesser importance, were to my mind in error. They ignored, as it were, the fact that the peasants' motives in joining such an organization sprang from their desire to realize a traditional value – namely, a higher income. In other words, the economic results of the organization determined the peasants' inclination to work for it.

It is interesting to note that in Tanzania too, another country where the government is seriously involved in persuading the peasants to join collective agricultural enterprises, there is much uncertainty with regard to the arguments which might persuade the peasants to mobilize. Conferences and seminars are arranged to discuss this question, but it remains a problem. The situation in Tanzania is not such that the peasants can be mobilized everywhere on the basis of class differences with any chance of success. This renders the situation all the more interesting, since the mobilisers are, as it were, seeking for what Lamond Tulis (1970) calls a 'structural bind',[2] a constraint that enforces unity.

In Chile, up to 1970, the most that could be found were tentative approaches to an ideology of co-operation; in the official and internal publications of INDAP for example, and among certain of its officials. At the outset INDAP had encouraged the small peasants to unite in neighbourhood committees; credit was then extended via these committees. It was only later, in 1968, that various neighbourhood committees were banded together into municipal and sometimes regional co-operatives. Table 9 gives some idea of the increase in the number of co-operatives.

Of the co-operatives in existence in December 1969, roughly 60% had less than 100 members and 20% more than 200.

There seemed to be several reasons why no clear ideology developed during the Frei period. Within the circles of the Christian-Democrats themselves opinions were divided on whether the small peasants ought to be integrated into the 'large' agricultural-economic system or whether a small-peasant economy ought to be created. This would

Table 9. Growth of small peasant co-operatives in Chile 1964–1969. Number of incorporated co-operatives (Cooperativas campesinas)

Year	1964	1965	1966	1967	1968	1969
Number of co-operatives	26	43	84	123	171	222
Number of members	1718	3204	7802	11452	18456	30034

involve forms of collective production with a vertical integration giving them their own supply firms, and selling organizations – in other words, their own market. This division also seemed to be linked with the fact that few people had any clear idea of how to set about organizing any of this. The peasants themselves were chiefly interested in economic improvements. In 1969 admittedly they had demanded land at practically every provincial congress, but only in the odd case did any individual co-operative exercise pressure on the government to expropriate a particular large farm. Until September 1970 at least it was only sporadically that a farm was indeed expropriated in favour of a co-operative. This mostly occurred in those provinces in which the leaders of the federation of co-operatives were most class-conscious, most convinced of the existence of a structural bind. By carrying out practically no expropriation in favour of the small, independent peasants, the government missed its chance to mobilize them in terms of this unifying constraint. This meant too that the co-operatives were more dependent upon government projects and credit than they might otherwise have been had they disposed of their own land. A further result was that the value of participation, of the peasants having a say in their own future, remained an empty slogan.

The most serious attempt – alongside some of the large projects – to achieve collective forms of production, was the issue of capital loans to smaller or larger groups, from 3 to 10 or more peasants. These groups were usually formed by co-option. Mostly the group ran a pig or chicken farm together, with each member having his own little farm on the side. Production groups with land, however, also occurred. The impression I retained after visiting such groups was that their cohesion and viability depended upon economic results. I shall discuss this point in more detail in the chapter on solidarity.

At this point it seems to me worthwhile to fill out what has already been said concerning the significance of leadership and management capacity and the chance of failure with a very detailed description of one particular case. Such descriptions are seldom given in sociological literature. Authors are usually satisfied with a brief summing up of factors which are supposed to explain why the project, or the co-operative as a whole, failed. Such a resumé, however, does not sufficiently impress upon the reader how closely these explanatory factors are connected and how slight is a project's chance of success in a developing country. To my mind this particular case has so many ideal-typical characteristics that it is well suited to serve as an illustration. It is certainly not a case which makes it easy for me to bolster up the assertions I have so far made. Chile was one of the most developed countries of Latin America; the Frei government was characterized by considerable sympathy for the peasants, and by honest attempts to assist their progress, while the technical standard of the Chilean official was no lower than that of officials elsewhere on the continent, on the contrary.

5.5 Case description

Our case concerns the regional cooperativa campesina of Calle Larga (pseudonym) which comprises several neighbourhood communities and lies under the smoke of a large city.

In 1966 a comparatively low ranking local official of INDAP came up with the idea of extending a large loan to the market-gardeners in the region. This would enable them to equip and organize a horticultural auction mart, which could serve as an alternative to the central market. This was situated in the large city, and dominated by large traders who exploited the market gardeners. (It is ideal-typical that the project was the brain-child of a local, comparatively low-ranking official). At this time the peasants were not even organized in a regional co-operative, but were scattered in small local, independent committees. For this reason a co-operative was first set up, before the loan was applied for. It was granted three years later, in September 1969. It was a large loan of $1\frac{1}{2}$ million escudos (rather more than £61,000). Both the provincial INDAP office and the local bureau appointed officials to get the project underway, certainly seven people in all. The team was headed by an agronomist.

During all this time the co-operative had been idle. About 200 peasants were by that time affiliated, but practically the only activity was the almost weekly meeting of the board which was sometimes attended by the delegates from the local committees. For almost two whole years the members of the board had met and tried to expedite the loan, without receiving anything in return. For this, thought INDAP, they deserved every credit. The chairman's capabilities were viewed with a more jaundiced eye – it was always the vice-chairman, for example, who took charge of the meetings while the chairman remained a bashful and silent spectator. When the chairman of the co-operative wished to appoint as business manager a woman who was a good friend of his, someone from INDAP made a counter proposal. After a fairly heated discussion – for the committee members regarded the proposal as a piece of authoritarian intervention on the part of INDAP – it was agreed to organize a sort of exam for those who wished to be considered for the paid post of business manager of the co-operative. This exam was in fact held in October or November of 1969. A member of the board and INDAP officials were there as invigilators, from 10 in the morning until 5 in the afternoon. Nine candidates had applied, including one delegate from a local committee of the co-operative. When, at 5 in the afternoon, the board member was already in the bus homeward bound, a tenth candidate suddenly made his appearance. He was from outside the city, had spent most of the day travelling and hadn't been able to get there any sooner. The INDAP officials decided that he too should be allowed to sit for the exam. He proved to head the list and the leader of the project wanted to appoint him. At the meeting which was to decide on the appointment of the manager the board members were extremely indignant over this state of affairs. They wanted no part of the man who had done best in the exam; they didn't know him. (This common standpoint had required some preparation. The one board member who had helped invigilate and felt extremely put out by the course events had taken, had called a secret board meeting – members of INDAP not admitted – and had won over the other members to his point of view.) For the sake of peace a decision was postponed; anyway the co-operative hadn't yet received any money from INDAP and could hardly pay a manager from an empty coffer. Meanwhile, in a number of meetings with the board and the delegates of the local committees, the INDAP officials had revealed the economic planning behind the project. There was a heated discussion about whether the co-operative ought indeed to deduct 16% of the product price for expenses. For produce brought to the central market one only paid $11\frac{1}{2}$% plus carriage, it was said. According to some of those present this difference meant that the peasants wouldn't deliver to the co-operative. The project estimated that the market-gardener members would deliver 35% of their crop to the co-operative in the first year, 50% the second year, 80% the third year and 100% the fourth year.

Few of those present were impressed by the argument that in this way they would build up the capital of their co-operative. If I die, said one of them, all my wife gets is my original investment plus 7% interest a year. In other words they would not be able to cash in on the capital growth. He didn't believe either that the co-operative would be able to obtain more for first class produce than was offered on the central market, even if it managed to obtain contracts with the large supermarkets in the city. He had sold to one of these enterprises from time to time and had never received more than the average market price.

Some did appreciate the argument that the co-operative might be able to use its capital to buy land for the members (urbanization in the region was progressing so rapidly that many members were in danger of losing their land and some had already lost part of it). Another member, though, didn't want the co-operative to plough back its profits into land, but would have preferred an expansion of the co-operative itself. (This suggestion came from someone who, before the Frei government, had benefitted by a local land reform carried out by the Catholic church).

No decisions were ever arrived at after such discussions; the meeting dispersed, the peasants thinking that INDAP would surely fix everything, the INDAP people worried by the egotism of the peasants. In October INDAP organized a two day course for the board members of the co-operative. Here too the same points came up for discussion and here too the peasants only partly understood the aim of the project, while the officials failed to realize that their explanation was falling short on some points. With regard to that 16% for expenses, for instance, INDAP stated that this was not a definite figure; if the peasants would deliver more than the expected quantities of produce, it could be lower (on a larger turnover). Nobody pointed out that it would not be known until the end of the year whether or not the peasants had delivered more than 35% of their crop, and that the 16% regulation would have to be retained for that year at least. Nevertheless these days – spent in Viña del Mar – were characterized by a certain cameraderie and solidarity among the participants.

Meanwhile, in October 1969, a large plot of land close to the city had been purchased. On it stood three long, but low, stone hen houses and also a large two-storeyed building, constructed entirely of stone, which resembled an engineering works. A civil engineer belonging to INDAP drew up plans of the alterations which would be necessary to convert the building into a covered market for receiving, sorting, packing and expediting market garden produce. Before the alterations had even begun a television team arrived from the city to film the event and give an account of the project. The agronomist in charge spent an entire morning leading them round.

As the board members had expected – although during a meeting with the INDAP people, who deplored their pessimism, they had finished up by offering their own services for the reconstruction job – the enthusiasm of the members, at least for helping with the alteration work, was not great. A few turned up during the first few weeks, on Saturdays and Sundays, but this was about all. Then, one fine day the co-operative started to pay those who showed up regularly for their work. The board had apparently decided, without informing INDAP, not to pay the volunteers 15 escudos in cash but to deduct this amount from their debt to the co-operative (few of the members had paid their admission dues in full). Students from the city also offered to help. This help was accepted at a meeting pregnant with political suspicion. Election time was coming up and the INDAP people were convinced that the students' main aim was to canvas within the co-operative. To the best of my knowledge they came only twice, both times on a Saturday.

A number of contractors were now engaged; one laid the water main – toilets were needed, among other things – while another put in the electricity. In January 1970 the co-operative received a brand-new truck, although as yet there was nothing they could use it for. It may have been this which inspired one of the lower, local INDAP officials, until the matter of reconstruction was finally settled, to propose to set up a sale-room for market-garden produce in a new suburb nearby. (The mayor had in fact already discussed this idea with the chairman of the co-operative.) If the municipality would let them have a piece of ground they could easily knock up an auction hall with the wood they already had plus a quantity of other material. (I was later informed that they were thinking in terms of 'three bags of cement and a kilo of nails'.) No sooner said than done. The municipality gave them the land. I do not know at what precise moment the leader of the project was informed of these plans; in any case, he should have been aware of them. While the alterations to the market hall ground to a halt, a bout of feverish activity was unleashed on the sale-room in the suburb. But, three months later, 28,000 escudos had already been spent on material for this enterprise which was supposed to cost almost nothing, and even then it wasn't completely finished. One reason for this was that the municipality – under the smoke of the great city, itself for the greater part urban – laid down certain requirements regarding the hygienic conditions of such a sale room. There was the additional factor that none of the members had any building experience.

In the midst of all this activity – in which the local INDAP personnel, three people in all, were daily and indeed very actively involved – a conflict broke out between the provincial INDAP authorities and these three. Two of them were suddenly transferred; the third remained in Calle Larga but was requested to have no more dealings with the co-operative. The reasons behind all this were complex in the extreme. One of the three had long ago incurred the displeasure of a powerful bigwig of INDAP in the province, who was linked with the PDC. His transfer had already been requested earlier but had been held up by the provincial director of INDAP who in his turn disliked the party man. One of the others, the one who had been allowed to remain in Calle Larga, was thought to be mixed up in politics. He was suspected of working for MAPU, the break-away ex-left wing of the Partido Democrata Cristiana. (In INDAP itself people were increasingly inclined to think in party political terms. Scarcely any attempt was made now to conceal the fact that one of the aims of the agency was to ensure Tomic's victory in the September 1970 elections. They were not yet openly canvassing for Tomic, but within the agency a start had been made on the muzzling of officials who were known or suspected to be anti-Tomic.) The blame for embarking on the sale-room project was laid at the door of the third official.

These three, who seemed to form a close-knit team, were also accused of criticizing the provincial INDAP people for mismanaging the project. They had complained too that the loan was doled out in dribs and drabs so that on one occasion there hadn't been enough money to pay the workmen. They had wanted nothing more to do with the local head of INDAP who, in his turn, was suspicious of his subordinates' insistence on a change in the board of the co-operative. He regarded it as a political manoeuvre in order to substitute kindred spirits. Their departure was a blow to the peasants – that is to say, the board of the co-operative. Harsh words were exchanged at the next meeting with the leader of the project. Even then it was not made clear who was now in charge: INDAP or the co-operative which had received the loan. Although the members of the board had switched jobs – the chairman had become acting manager of the co-operative and also drove the truck, for which he received 1800 escudos per month; the vice-chairman had been made chairman; the secretary had been dismissed for not attending meetings and replaced by an acting board member (a suplente) – this had done nothing to improve their shilly-shallying and lack of expertise. INDAP would have liked to have seen them all replaced, but this was not legally possible until the general meeting had approved the balance sheets for the past two years. These balance sheets, however, had still to be made up and passed by the Ministry of Economic Affairs . . .

(The situation seemed almost nightmarish to an outsider who happened to be a sociologist. I found it unbelievable, for instance, that in all those months it had not been established who was in charge and that the agronomist from INDAP, who put in an appearance once or twice a week, could carry on as though merely a few trifling difficulties were involved. Yet the peasants too persisted in their role; they too professed not to see that the project was beyond them. If the chairman of the control commission of the co-operative, Don Lucho, whose carping voice was heard at almost every meeting, stated in plain terms that the management was incompetent, the members took this criticism personally, lost their tempers and simply threatened to resign. Constructive criticism in the sense of discussing how a thing should be done and who should do it, was almost impossible. No agenda was ever drawn up for the meetings; it was more a permanent question and answer session. This tended to mean that, before one subject had been properly discussed, people had already passed on to the next.)

At around this time, the INDAP project leader, the agronomist, went abroad for six weeks. (The curtain had already fallen when he returned, but this doesn't seem to have caused him any trouble; his failure degenerated into a quarrel between his direct boss and the provincial director of INDAP.) He was replaced by a young book-keeper. This man and the official in charge of social affairs had the courage to raise the alarm, thus compelling the highest INDAP officials in the province to come to a decision. Although as late as March 1970 yet another investigation commission from the national INDAP office had returned home satisfied, after a visit to the co-operative, now, scarcely a month later, the details had to be scrutinized. It appeared that the unauthorized saleroom had already cost 28,000 escudos, and was going to cost more. It appeared that the truck, which had cost nearly 100,000 escudos, had hardly earned a penny in four months. It appeared that not one of the board members knew how much credit, in cash, the co-operative had so far received from INDAP (around 130,000 escudos). Meanwhile the co-operative had begun selling in the new suburb. The results were hardly spectacular, just sufficient to pay the salary of the salesman appointed by the co-operative, although this was hard to work out exactly. The manager worked with one big cashbox, from which he took money when he went to buy produce, returning to it in the evening whatever was left, plus the proceeds of the sale-room. Yet even at the meeting where all this emerged the board insisted at the end that they alone, without the INDAP people, would decide what was to be done.

They managed to keep things going for a time and at a later meeting even converted the highest INDAP officers in the province to the extent that they began to blame themselves, and each other, for the failure. The oddest rumours circulated at the INDAP office in the city. It was said, for instance, that the provincial director belonged to an opposition party and had been ordered to sabotage the project. Every rumour seemed reasonable, evidently, in the rarefied political atmosphere of that early summer of 1970; besides, it was an excellent means of obscuring where the real responsibility lay. The co-operative appointed a new manager, who even drew up an alternative project, i.e. that the co-operative should start a mixing installation for cattle fodder and should trade in non-perishable agrarian products.

But INDAP had washed its hands of the whole idea. No more credit was extended and in July 1970 the plot, with the market building still only party reconstructed, was rented to a metal construction firm. The suburban saleroom was still functioning but the purchases for this were made in, of all places, the city, at the central market. The quantities sold were too small to interest the market-gardening members. In August the co-operative was still employing seven men, but was no longer able to pay their salaries (11,000 escudos per month). The end was near.

5.6 Postscript

It appears much more difficult to mobilize small peasants who do not have to cope with a common local opponent than to organize those who do. With the latter, the purpose is to end local exploitation, but with the independent peasants there is the much more arduous task of improving their position within a national economic system. It is hoped to achieve this by means of an association which at the same time must realize other aims, such as a greater participation in decision making and a greater degree of equality. I shall return to the problems posed by this in later chapters, particularly in the chapter which deals with solidarity. However, I hope that I have already made it clear that these problems are sizeable. They spring on the one hand from the underdevelopment of the country: lack of capital, lack of management capacity and expertise among both peasants and government, a lack of solidarity among the peasants. On the other hand problems arise from the fact that the co-operative, as an institution, is expected to accomplish a number of aims which often remain merely implied and are, to some extent, conflicting. In view of this the failure of so many agricultural co-operatives in the Third World is hardly surprising.

Chapter 6 Members and non-members of associations

6.1 Introduction

In the preceding chapters we have dealt mainly with the structural variables which determined the mobilization of peasants and agricultural labourers at the level of the local community and of society. Our findings were based upon the relevant literature and the results of qualitative research. We also linked the degree of involvement of the agricultural workers in rural syndicates with specific traits of the agrarian structure, with the aid of figures derived from the Chilean agricultural census. However, before going on to examine the problems arising in these associations once established, we shall first consider the differences between members and non-members of syndicates and co-operatives. In other words we shall descend to the level of the *individual*. We wish to discover if there is any systematic difference between members and non-members, if there is a particular type of person who joined these associations. The preliminary research led us to expect that this was indeed so. In the following sections we shall review our hypotheses regarding the differences between members and non-members, dealing first with the syndicates and then with the co-operatives. We shall then discuss the results obtained from an analysis of the survey data.

6.2 The syndicates

6.2.1 Hypotheses

The basic hypothesis underlying the survey among members and non-members of farming syndicates in Chile was that there were four motives which might lead workers to affiliate.
These were:
1. The worker might appreciate the utility, the instrumental, especially economic value, of the syndicate.
2. The worker might have joined because he valued and wanted to maintain the interaction with his friends, relatives or acquaintances who were already members.
3. The worker might have joined out of a sense of obligation, of solidarity with his peers; responding to a norm of solidarity which demands unity.
4. He might have been coerced into joining.
The fourth motive did not hold good in Chile, so I did not pursue it. A survey in the United States (Hagstrom & Selvin, 1965) had shown that the various indicators of cohesion between members of associations could be reduced to two factors, instrumental and sociometric appreciation, corresponding to motives 1 and 2 of my hypotheses. I could

also imagine, however, and certainly in the case of syndicates, i.e. militant class organizations, that a person might join not primarily because membership could be useful to him, nor because he valued the companionship of the other members, but because he felt that he must make common cause, show solidarity with those others who shared the same socio-economic position as himself, or because a norm required this of him.

Looking back it seems to me that motives 2 and 3 are both based on solidarity among members of the same group. What I was not so quick to notice was that the act of joining, born of solidarity, may be done gladly or with some reluctance, under pressure of the social control of the other members of the group. An act of solidarity may also spring from the sense of identification mentioned in the third motive, but not in the case of members of the same, yet comparatively small, group. In such a group identification must go hand in hand with relationships and, if there is any question of solidarity at all, people either join associations automatically because the others join, or under social pressure.

We have thus three motives which, for convenience sake, may be termed 'utility of the association', 'attraction of interaction' and 'obedience to a norm'. I assumed that these motives, in their turn, would depend upon various other factors and variables.

With regard to *utility*, I reasoned as follows. To appreciate the possible value of the farming syndicate the worker must cease to link his interest with that of the owner. He would also need to be aware of his social-economic situation. In more concrete terms this led me to postulate the following hypotheses and sub-hypotheses. In comparison with the non-member, the member will

1   have less of a patronage relationship with the owner (cf. Urzua, 1969, p. 122), because, for example, he

1.1   depends less upon the owner since he is younger and has a smaller family;

1.2   has had less opportunity to build up a relationship since he has not lived there so long;

1.3   is more dissatisfied from the economic point of view (experiences a greater relative deprivation); or

1.4   earns less than the non-member.

The member will, in comparison with the non-member

2   be more aware of his situation (believe less in the possibility of social climbing) because for instance

2.1   he is better educated;

2.2   has had more contact with urban culture;

2.3   has more often worked elsewhere.

Regarding the *attraction of interaction* motive, I postulated that in the first place relations based on friendship and family ties would coincide with membership and not cut across it. The hypotheses in question were:

3   that the member will have more friends and relatives among the other members of the syndicate than among the non-members. The reverse is true of the non-members.

It might also be expected that

4   the frequency of interaction would be higher among members than among non-members (operationalized as: more often participating in large work groups).

Turning to psychology (Schachter, 1961) I added the hypothesis that

5   the member would experience greater anxiety (operationalized as: would more often be the eldest son).

Schachter had indeed found that people suffering from anxiety need to seek the company of others in the same circumstances. He also found that the same kind of situation aroused greater anxiety among first-born and thus a greater affiliation.

Regarding the *solidarity norm* which had led the members to affiliate I drew up the following hypotheses. These refer to the circumstances under which such a norm might be expected to exercise more influence. In comparison with the non-member I expected that the member

6   would be of a more religious disposition;
7   would more often have an affective primary relationship outside his family or kin group and would thus
7.1   more often have a good friend outside the family circle;
7.1   more often have been one of a group of friends in his youth[1];
8   place less value upon relationships with relatives and members of the immediate family;
9   be more keen on co-operation or more likely to consider co-operation necessary;
10   be more sensitive to the opinion of his peers (McClelland, 1961, p. 186 ff.);
11   identify more with the other workers on the fundo and with the campesinos (peasants) in general;
12   give less evidence of the conception called by Foster (1965) the Image of Limited Good, the idea that one person progresses at the expense of another.

6.2.2   Results

The data provided by surveys among members and non-members of syndicates on the nine fundos mentioned in Chapter 2 confirm many of our hypotheses. It would, however, be excessive to reproduce all the frequency classifications here since this would require over twenty tables[2]. In presenting the results of the comparison between members and non-members I shall retain the sequence of hypotheses employed above. Regarding the motives underlying affiliation, the anthropological survey had already shown that a large majority of members had been led to join the organization because of its instrumental value. The open survey question concerning their motive in affiliating was codified according to the most important component of the reply, as follows:

	%	N
Improvement of living standard through the organization	27	38
More certainty regarding possibility of permanent employment	11	16
Putting an end to abuse and arbitrary powers of employer, forming a countervailing power	25	36
Under pressure of workmates	18	26
At the invitation of friends	15	22
Other reasons	3	5
Total	100	143

We see that 38% of the replies refer to the usefulness of the organization to the individual respondent; a further 25% refer to this usefulness but in terms which evoke the class character of the organization. Of the respondents 33% gave a reply which indicated that the friendly or less friendly social control of others had been of significance. Everything would seem to indicate that all three of our expected motives played a role.

We assumed that the utility motive resulted from a weakening of the traditional patronage relationship between owner and worker and from the worker's greater awareness of his true position.

Hypothesis 1: the member has less of a patronage relationship with the owner. We did indeed find that the member scored lower on the patronage index than the non-member, which confirmed the hypothesis. In concrete terms, this implied that the non-member was more often of the opinion that the owner of the fundo helped his workers (instead of doing nothing for them or being prejudicial to them). Also, when asked whom he would approach in order to borrow 100 escudos he was more likely to mention the owner. Table 10 shows the difference in patronage orientation. To what must it be ascribed?

As expected the non-members had a somewhat larger number of financial dependents than did the members. There was, however, no age difference between the two categories. Furthermore, it appeared that the non-members had been living on the fundo somewhat longer than the members, although the association was very weak. However, the non-members had started to work earlier on the fundo, in comparison with the members. There seemed to be no connection, though, between membership and size of salary. Nor was it clear whether the members were more dissatisfied with the size of their salary than the non-members. We found that 58% of the members as against 46% of the non-members considered a just wage to be a sum at least 50% higher than the existing wage. Sub-hypothesis 1.1 and 1.2 were thus partly confirmed, while 1.3 and 1.4 were not.

Table 10.   Membership of syndicates and patronage (%)

	Patronage index				N
	1 (low)	2	3	4 (high)	
Members	7	23	43	27	143
Non-members	1	7	39	52	67
Total	5	18	42	35	210

χ^2 (3 d.f.) = 17.65[1]

1 The respondents did not constitute a random sample, as was explained in Chapter 2. There is accordingly no question of applying statistical tests to determine whether a difference in the sample may be put down to a difference inherent in the population. Nonetheless, even when interviewing a population, some of the differences found may be due to errors in measuring or punching and not to actual differences in that population. A criterion is therefore necessary in order to determine that a particular difference is too large to be attributed to errors in measurement or any other cause. I used as my criterion the 5% significance level of the χ-square. After all, the χ-square is also an association standard of measurement.

Hypothesis 2 assumed among members a greater awareness of and insight into their own situation, and I did indeed find a number of indications for this. Asked for his view on how Chilean land reform ought to be carried out, the member was more inclined than the non-member to mention structural changes (31% as against 22%). He also tended to reply more frequently that communal forms of production would have to follow expropriation (15% v. 6%). The answers to both open questions revealed furthermore that the member thought more often in terms of collaboration between peasants than did the non-members (36% v. 18%). More often too the member viewed the function of the syndicate in terms of striving to promote land reform (17% v. 9%). Other data might also serve to show that the members had more insight into the necessity for reform and co-operation. A question regarding their preference for a piece of land of their own, participation in communal farming or good wages provided the surprising result shown in Table 11. The members would prefer a piece of land of their own while the non-members are well satisfied with a good wage.

In the first instance neither category seems very enthusiastic about the communal farm, the asentamiento, which arose out of the Chilean land reform. Matters were different with regard to the second choice, mentioned in Table 12; the asentamiento proved a real alternative for the members, whereas the non-members still seemed pretty lukewarm.

Although the percentage of members displaying insight remained low in all the variables mentioned, it was always higher than that of the non-members. However, when

Table 11.   Preferences of members and non-members of syndicates (first choice)

	Own piece of land		Participation in asentamiento		Good wage	
	%	N	%	N	%	N
Members	67	96	8	11	25	36
Non-members	44	30	1	1	54	36
Total	60	126	6	12	34	72

χ^2 (2 d.f.) = 17.72

Table 12.   Preferences of members and non-members of syndicates (second choice)

	Own piece of land		Participation in asentamiento		Good wage	
	%	N	%	N	%	N
Members	25	36	25	36	48	69
non-members	48	32	12	8	39	26
Total	32	68	21	44	45	95

χ^2 (2 d.f.) = 10.4

asked if they thought it possible that 'a peasant like themselves' could progress in life, the categories did not differ at all: 72% of the members and 70% of the non-members thought that he could. Nonetheless I consider Hypothesis 2 to a large extent confirmed.

We assumed that the greater insight on the part of the members would go hand in hand with a higher degree of education. The data did indeed indicate that the members were somewhat better educated. Of the members, 57% (as against 42% of the non-members) had gone higher than the 3rd class in the primary school. The association, however, is weak. I considered that another possibility for acquiring more insight into one's own situation might lie in having worked elsewhere, on another fundo. Table 13 shows the results. It is striking that both categories worked just as frequently on another fundo in the same community, i.e. close to the pesent fundo, but that the members had worked much more often outside their present community. Given the fact that the non-members were more often involved in a patronage-relationship with the owner, and had worked less often on another farm, it is not surprising that more non-members than members considered the farm on which they were employed to be better to work on than any other farm (58% v. 40%).

This showed that, as we had assumed, affiliation is largely connected with a weakening of the patronage relationship and, to a lesser degree, with a better insight into one's own situation.

The second affiliation motive, the attraction of interaction with other workers on the farm, proved earlier to have played a real role. Let us now view the position with regard to the hypotheses derived from this motive.

Hypothesis 3 postulated that friendships and family ties would not conflict with membership.

The replies show a very clear link between membership of a syndicate and friendly relationships. The member has friends who are also members while the friends of the non-members are not themselves members either.

Exactly the same is true of the kinship relationships between members, non-members and others working on the same fundo. The relatives of the member are usually members themselves; those of the non-members are frequently not affiliated. However, members and non-members have the same proportion of relatives *living* on the same fundo.

Table 13. Frequency of work elsewhere (%)

| | Worked on another fundo | | | |
	outside present community	within present community	Didn't work on other fundo	N
Members	21	31	48	143
Non-members	5	30	65	66
Total	16	31	53	209

χ^2 (2 d.f.) = 10.38

Table 14. Membership and friendship[1]

| | Friends | | | |
	both members (%)	one a member (%)	neither member (%)	N
Members	67	23	9	141
Non-members	15	27	58	59
Total	52	25	23	200

χ^2 (2 d.f.) = 63.44

1 Earlier in the interview the respondent was asked for the names of his two best friends among the other workers on the fundo. The table refers to the membership of these two persons.

Table 15. Membership and kinship

| | Relatives are | | | |
	all members (%)	some members (%)	none members (%)	N
Members	45	42	13	100
Non-members	10	51	39	51
Total	33	45	22	151

χ^2 (2 d.f.) = 23.86

Tables 14 and 15 indicate how pronounced these differences are. This serves to prove hypothesis 3.

We assumed that the members would display a more frequent interaction than the non-members. The only available indicator in this connection is the size of the person's normal workgroup and this did indeed appear somewhat larger among the members. *Hypothesis 4* seems acceptable, yet we cannot consider it proved by this one indicator.

The hypothesis derived from Schachter, according to which affiliation might result from a greater anxiety, was not confirmed, at least not so far as regards the indicator I employed. Both members and non-members seemed just as frequently to be the eldest sons of their parents (24% as against 28%).

The third motive we assumed was obedience to a norm of solidarity, responding to social pressure from the other workers on the fundo. From the replies to the question regarding the motive underlying affiliation one might conclude that solidarity under pressure of social control had indeed played a role for some. However, the member did not seem to be of a more religious disposition, as assumed by *Hypothesis 6*. When asked which of two opinions best represented their own standpoint, 76% of the members and 80% of the non-members identified with the peasant in whose life religion assumed an important role.

As we have already mentioned, *Hypotheses 7.1* and *7.2* were derived from the study made by Bonilla and Silva Michelena in Venezuela. They found that, in comparison with non-members, rural syndicate members were more likely to have an intimate friend outside the extended family circle and to have been one of a group of friends in their youth. On the basis of these differences they assumed that the member had already had more socializing experiences which would prepare him for solidary interaction with non-related peers. Both these hypotheses were confirmed during our research in Chile. We found that 53 % of the members as against 30 % of the non-members had an intimate friend who was not a relative and 58 % of the members, compared with 39 % of the non-members, had formed one of a group of intimate friends during his lifetime.

The data indicate that when asked to classify a number of groups according to how close they felt to them, the members valued their relatives on average somewhat lower than the non-members. The averages were 3.38 compared with 3.08 on a scale running from 1 up to and including 7. However, the difference is not large enough for us to consider the hypothesis in question confirmed.

The members appeared more ready than non-members to work their regalias – the small pieces of land made available to them as part of their wages – as one piece, in a communal effort (64 % against 45 %). Other indications that members were more inclined than non-members to consider co-operation necessary, or to think in terms of co-operation, have already been mentioned in connection with hypothesis 2. *Hypothesis 9*, postulating that members were more ready to collaborate, seems confirmed.

Sensitivity to the opinion of peers, a factor regarded by McClelland (1961) as extremely important for the development of solidarity, was measured by means of two conflicting statements on how the speaker would react to criticism voiced at a meeting. The respondents were asked which statement best reflected their opinion. The members did indeed state less often than the non-members (30 % as against 48 %) that they would not accept this criticism, thus showing themselves, as we expected, to be more sensitive to the opinion of their peers.

Identification with the workers on the fundo and with the peasants in general was measured with the aid of a question to which we have already referred, i.e. arranging a number of groups in the order in which they appealed to the respondent. Although in both cases the members have a somewhat lower average score (3.67 compared with 3.80 and 3.94 as against 4.46) and therefore identify a trifle more with the two categories mentioned, the differences are not such that we may regard the hypothesis as clearly confirmed.

We expected the members to be less inclined to view the world as a struggle of all against all in which one could progress only at the expense of someone else. Foster (1965) and other anthropologists after him, thought that this view of the world was typical of underdeveloped peasant communities. In some cases this Image of the Limited Good is no more than a hard-headed view of what really happens, as we were able to observe in Chapter 3 when discussing the functions of patronage. As a general attitude, however, this Image exercises an unfavourable influence upon solidarity within the peasant community. The respondents were asked which of two conflicting opinions most approximated to their own. One opinion held that one peasant could usually only progress at the expense of the others, the other assertion contradicted this. We found that 18 % of the members and 34% of the non-members considered that the progress of one was usually at the expense of the others. The hypothesis that the non-members adhere more often to the Image of Limited Good appears confirmed.

6.2.3   The member: an ideal-typical portrait

From the hypotheses confirmed in the foregoing section a certain picture of the member emerges. Clearly, in comparison with the non-member, he is more detached from the patronage link with the owner and adopts a more critical attitude towards the latter. This is partly because he can permit himself to be more critical, being somewhat less dependent. There appear, for instance, to be more inquilinos among the first members than among the later ones (62%, 52% and 31% of those who became members in or before 1967, in 1968 and in or after 1969 respectively, were inquilinos). It would seem that, as we assumed in Chapter 3, those peasants with a somewhat greater degree of economic security were the first to affiliate. Admittedly they were not secure against reprisals but at the same time the owner could not abruptly refuse them work as he could with the voluntarios. The member can be more critical too, because he has more often worked elsewhere and thus has material for comparison. He has more insight into his own situation and appreciates better the necessity for agricultural workers to co-operate. The differences between him and the non-member are not great; for the member too relationships with family and friends remain important, so important indeed that they seldom conflict with membership. *This indicates that affiliation is not so much an individual as a collective decision taken within family and friendly groups.*

More often than the non-member, the member has passed through a certain socialization process with groups of friends. This leaves him more open to ties of intimate friendship with people other than relatives and also makes him more sensitive to the opinion of others. However, this does not mean that members have a great deal of confidence in their fellow men. The last piece of advice given by 80% of the members and 85% of the non-members to a migrating son would be not to put too much trust in other people. However, it may well be that members do place more reliance on their fellow men within the fundo.

The utility motive is of primary importance. The members joined because they expected advantages from the syndicate, even if their decision was taken only after consultation with family and friends. It appeared, accordingly, that in February 1970 the non-members were not so sure of the syndicate's success as were the members. Although 42% (as against 93% of the members) thought that the syndicate had achieved considerable success, the majority was not so convinced. It may be, though, that this can be attributed in part to the policy of the owners who were often said to favour the non-members, giving them lighter work and treating them better. This meant that the latter profited from the presence of a syndicate by not becoming members.

The survey was carried out on nine different fundos in three comunas. The numbers are too small to determine whether those hypotheses which were confirmed held good for all the fundos. I did, however, examine whether this was true of each comuna. There did appear to be differences, in the sense that in a particular comuna the associations generally found appeared so weak that, relying on my chi-square criterion, I found it impossible to arrive at any conclusion. The variables associated with affiliation in all three comunas are: the indicators concerning the intensity of the patronage relationship with the owner, the smaller number of people financially dependent on the respondent, among the members; the more favourable view of the syndicate's success among the members and the fact that affiliation and relationships with family or friends do not conflict. This confirms the most important features of the portrait sketched above. The member is more convinced of the utility of the syndicate and has detached himself more from the patron than has the non-member, for he is less dependent upon him. The decision to join is evidently a collective one and is taken in consultation with family and friends.

6.2.4   The non-members

Although I have thus far depicted them as one category, the non-members really consist of two categories, the ex-members and the never-members. Particularly in the fundo San Manuel we encountered workers who had once been affiliated. Here a large number of workers had left the syndicate during a labour conflict because they felt they had been deceived by their leaders. Ex-members however were also encountered on other fundos.[3]

How did these ex-members differ from those who had never been members? The quantitative data show that the ex-members have worked longer on the fundo and are older than the never-members. They are also, more frequently, head of a family.

It is not clear whether their resignation was the result or the cause of the peculiar nature of their family relationships. The ex-members place a significantly higher value on their family and relatives than do either the members or never-members. They are less prepared than the never-members to work their regalias in common, are more attached to their own property and are quicker to see the difficulties arising from co-operation. They are, however, less influenced than the never-members by the Image of the Limited Good (23% against 47%). From all this a picture emerges of someone afraid of being put upon by non-relatives and who has probably felt taken in before. He is more alive to the practical problems posed by co-operation. The ex-member states more often than the never-member (20% as against 3%) that he hasn't a single friend on the fundo and he is less likely than the never-member to have friends within the syndicate. This despite the fact that he has compadres more frequently than does the never-member. This isolation may result in part from his resignation from the syndicate; he may now be looked at askance by his former friends. However, it seems also to be partly due to a lack of experience of being on friendly terms with social peers outside the circle of relatives. On this point there is no difference between ex-members and never-members. This same lack may have played a part in his resignation, which was often preceded by a conflict. It may also lie at the root of his reluctance to relinquish some of his independence for the sake of co-operating with others. The reasons given for resigning, categorized on the basis of replies to an open question, were as follows:

	%	N
Conflicts with the board or members of the syndicate	31	11
Desire to improve relations with the owner	18	6
The syndicate was no longer useful to him	20	7
He didn't agree with the objectives	15	5
Other reasons	20	7

76

This shows that the reasons lie partly in the domain of personal relationships with the other members of the organization, with the consequent necessity for accepting a compromise, and partly in a greater dependence on the owner, whose favour is felt to sway one's own fortunes. Although this may have been due to spite, it is nonetheless remarkable that the ex-members took a less positive view of the syndicate's success than did the never-members. During the anthropological part of the research I heard of cases of syndicate leaders who were, so to speak, bought out by the owner of the farm on which they worked, with promotion or a larger regalia. No such case occurred in our inquiry but it is probable that our ex-members too, or some of them at least, will have had a nudge from the owner.

6.2.5 Multiple correlation

In order to test the adequacy of the variables included in my hypotheses and thus in the survey, we have calculated how much of the variance in membership can be explained by a number of these variables taken together.

The computation identified eight important variables which together explained 60% of the variance in affiliation. A somewhat surprising revelation is the considerable influence seemingly exercised by relationship with friends. This comes about in two ways. On the one hand people ensure that affiliation does not cut across ties of friendship, which can only be done by mutual consultation before joining[4]. On the other the members have evidently undergone a socializing process in the maintenance of relationships with people outside the family. They have intimate friends, they are more sensitive to criticism and they are less inclined to believe that one person progresses at the expense of the others.

In addition they believe in the advantages generated by the syndicate, are more aware of the necessity for collective forms of production after expropriation and think less well of the owner. They have a wider vision, perhaps also because they have worked elsewhere.

Table 16. Cumulative squared multiple correlation coefficient R^2 with membership of the syndicate. N = 195

Variable	R^2	T-value	Fraction explained	Partial correlation coefficient
Affiliation of friends	0.32	9.14	0.18	0.56
View of the success of the syndicate	0.45	5.65	0.07	0.38
View on land reform	0.50	4.02	0.035	0.28
Has intimate friend, not related	0.52	3.44	0.025	0.24
Patronage (opinion of owner)	0.54	3.09	0.02	−0.22
Sensitivity to the opinion of peers	0.56	2.82	0.02	0.21
Image of Limited Good	0.58	2.82	0.02	−0.20
Having worked elsewhere	0.60	2.67	0.01	0.19

6.3   The Co-operatives

6.3.1   Introduction

From the very outset of the Frei government in Chile, INDAP also turned its attention to the development of the small, independent peasant-farmers who had no direct local opponent to react against but who were nonetheless poor. If the official ideology regarded the agricultural workers as future participants in a communal farming enterprise run by themselves, the Leitbild for the peasant-farmers was also one of co-operation. To begin with INDAP encouraged them to become members of a local committee which was intended to have some control over the local distribution of the credit extended by INDAP. In practice this amounted to INDAP refusing credit to non-members, with the committee perhaps exercising a certain social control. They could advise INDAP to refuse credit to peasants who had a bad name locally and they could warn defaulters to pay off their loans.

After a few years it became obvious that these committees were too small to raise any sort of sizeable capital. INDAP then decided to incorporate the local committees in municipal – and in some cases regional – co-operatives. The committee members were encouraged to join these co-operatives and many did so, although membership involved a slight financial sacrifice. The motives behind affiliation, and the factors which, in their turn, might influence these motives, differed somewhat from those which led people to join a syndicate. The most important difference was that the small peasant-farmers were not obliged to break off or at least tone down a patronage relationship before being able to join. For the rest, however, I assumed that members of co-operatives had similar reasons for joining as did the members of syndicates. The utility motive in particular played an important role, as our reconnaissance showed. Here and there, though, I came across peasants, particularly board members of co-operatives, who appeared to be aware of the need for solidarity. They realized that, generally speaking, small peasant-farmers, working as individuals, had no chance of raising their standard of living. They saw that it was essential to co-operate and some of them had reached the conclusion that it was up to them to bring about this co-operation.

6.3.2   Hypotheses

It seemed to me that there could be two reasons for appreciating the possible *utility* of a co-operative, more insight and understanding or a greater objective need for the services which the co-operative could provide. I therefore assumed that, with regard to the question of insight, the members, in comparison with non-members, would have:
1.1   had more education;
1.2   come to know other behavioural alternatives (through more contact with urban culture);
1.3   more often worked elsewhere;
1.4   more modern farming methods (be more likely to keep accounts);
1.5   greater confidence in future possibilities for the small peasant-farmer.
Insofar as insight is based upon objective needs, it may be expected that the members
2.1   had larger farms than the non-members;

2.2   were more likely to own their land.

Finally, it could be that the members were more keenly aware of the possible utility of the co-operative because they felt poorer than other peasants. In comparison with non-members

3   members would feel relatively more deprived.

In the case of the co-operatives too, which had, after all, grown out of local committees and which still had the local communities as their basic unit of recruitment, it was quite possible that a person might become a member not so much because he was keenly aware of the advantages, but because his friends or relatives had joined. Regarding the *attraction of interaction motive*, I postulated the following hypotheses:

4.1   Members will have friends who are also members, non-members friends who are not.

4.2   Members will have relatives who are themselves members of the co-operative; non-members relatives who are not members either.

4.3   Members will interact more frequently with other peasants in the community than will non-members.

4.4   Members will identify more with the community (will more often say that there is more friendship there than in other communities).

The *solidarity norm* might also play a role, arising from a feeling of traditional attachment to the other peasants in the community. In such a case the members might, in comparison with non-members

5.1   be more religious;

5.2   more often be (have been) one of a group of friends;

5.3   more often have a good friend outside the family circle;

5.4   value relationships with immediate family and relatives less, those with the community relatively more;

5.5   be more likely to apply the traditional form of co-operation, of mutual help (vuelta de mano) on the land.

This solidarity, as the preliminary investigation showed, might also be based upon the realization that co-operation is essential if the standard of living of the small peasant-farmer is to be improved. It might then be expected

6.1   that the members would have more insight into the necessity for small peasant-farmers to co-operate;

6.2   that members would be more inclined to favour co-operation (participation in a communal farm);

6.3   that members would be more sensitive to the opinion of social peers;

6.4   that members would be less inclined to regard social equals as rivals (would not think that one peasant can only progress at the expense of others).

6.3.3   Results

The survey confirmed that the utility motive was the most important. To an open question regarding their motives for membership which explicitly inquired about other motives, 64 % of the members replied in terms which indicated that they had only joined the co-operative for the services it offered. A further 19 % gave as their reason the hope of receiving capital credit via the co-operative. Only 17 % answered in such a way as to suggest that they realized the necessity of co-operation for small peasant-farmers. The non-members shared these views: 85% of them thought that members joined, hoping to benefit from credit and other forms of support, while 40% gave as their own reason for not joining the fact that they didn't see the use of it and just weren't interested. Another 16% said that they had no money to pay the dues; 20% were unaware that the co-operative existed or had been too lazy to enroll and finally, 17% wanted to see how things went but in principle felt little enthusiasm for a co-operative.

From these replies one can only deduce that alongside the predominant utility motive, there were a number of members who realized the necessity for co-operation. The replies showed no evidence of the attraction of interaction. If we review the hypotheses concerning the greater insight into reality possessed by members, it appears that the members: are rather more likely than non-members to have had a secondary education (17.5% as against 10%) and to claim that they are good at reading (61% v. 48%). However, the differences are not such that we can consider the hypothesis proved (the chi-square which we are once again using as association yardstick only becomes 'significant' within a margin of uncertainty of roughly 15%). The hypothesis does, however, appear probable.

The same holds good for contact with the city. In the three months before the survey members visited the city somewhat more frequently than non-members (59% of the members as against 50% of the non-members), but the difference is too slight to confirm the hypothesis.

Rather more of the members had previously worked elsewhere (54% v. 45%), but once again the difference is too small to serve as confirmation of our hypothesis. As regards the keeping of accounts, which I used as an indicator of modernity unconnected with the degree of prosperity, there appeared to be no difference at all between members and non-members.

In keeping with Hypothesis 1.5 the members seem somewhat more optimistic concerning the future prospects of the small peasant-farmer. In fact, 49% of the members as against 28% of the non-members think that it is still possible for a smallholder to make progress. Hypothesis 1.5 is thus proved. Table 17 shows the differences. One might postulate that those who think that a small peasant-farmer *can* make progress alone would in fact not become members of a co-operative, in other words that the hypothesis should have been reversed. This argument would be correct if it were true that affiliation in fact

Table 17. Confidence in the future prospects of small peasant farmers among members and non-members of co-operatives in %

	A small peasant farmer can make progress alone				
	yes	under certain circumstances	not unless assisted	no	N
Members	28	21	21	29	182
Non-members	15	13	19	52	92
Total	24	19	20	37	274

χ^2 (3 d.f.) = 14.90

depended upon insight into the necessity for co-operation. The motives listed above, however, showed that this was not so: people are much more inclined to become members for the sake of the economic advantages for each individual peasant. The co-operative is regarded as a means of realizing an individual aim, namely the progress of one's own farm.

The slight differences in education and in contact with the urban culture (Hypotheses 1.1 and 1.2) might in their turn result from a difference in status. So too, having more land, working a larger farm, in short, experiencing an objectively greater need for the services offered by a co-operative might lead to a better insight into its advantages. The data show that members dispose of slightly more irrigated land (Table 18). The difference, however, is so slight that this factor can hardly be assumed to have played an important role in affiliation; only 53 % of the members, as against 55 % of the non-members had such land. With regard to non-irrigated – but tillable – land, there is no difference between members and non-members. Concerning the third category of land, cerro, which I distinguished, i.e. strongly sloping unirrigated land, marginal for agriculture, there is no

Table 18. Partition (%) of irrigated land among members and non-members of co-operatives[1]. 1 cuadra = 1.56 ha

	< 1 cuadra	$\geqslant 1 < 2$ cuadra	$\geqslant 2 < 5$ cuadra	$\geqslant 5 < 10$ cuadra	$\geqslant 10$ cuadra	N
Members	13	18	43	19	8	102
Non-members	21	29	31	15	4	52
Total	17	21	39	17	6	154

χ^2 (4 d.f.) = 5.98

1 Respondents with no irrigated land are not included.

Table 19. Tenure status of members and non-members of co-operatives composed of small peasant-farmers in %[1].

	Farmland is			
	owned	partly owned	not owned	N^1
Members	40	12	48	171
Non-members	33	11	55	87
Total	38	12	50	258

χ^2 (2 d.f.) = 1.26

1 The members and non-members who did not cultivate land, for whatever reason (11 members and 5 non-members) are not included in the table.

difference in average, although there is in distribution. Members more frequently have less or more cerro than non-members. All in all, the data do not confirm the hypothesis. At best they show that it is not absurd and that in other cases this factor may indeed play an important role, as postulated in Chapter 5 with the ideal typical description of co-operatives. Table 19 shows that members and non-members seem scarcely to differ in tenure status. What slight difference there is tends in the predicted direction.

It seems to me that affiliation cannot be explained by a difference in tenure status – and thus an objective need for a co-operative.

I asked the respondents what seemed to them a fair and just income for the work they did and how much more they would have to earn in order to attain that income. It appeared that, although the members regard a somewhat higher income as a just reward, the non-members earn less than the members and would themselves have to earn more in order to attain this just income. The non-members feel more relative deprivation than the members (expressed as a percentual rise in the income necessary to achieve an income thought of as just). Table 20 shows this. Accordingly, Hypothesis 3 appears incorrect: it is the non-members who feel more deprived.

The hypotheses dealt with so far show that the difference between members and non-members regarding insight into the advantages of a co-operative is not so much one of status (education or size of farm) but rather of mentality. Members take a more optimistic view of the future prospects of small peasant-farmers; they feel somewhat less deprived than non-members and also appear to be a little further along the road towards becoming employers in a small way. Not only do they earn rather more, they also want to earn more than do the non-members. This mentality seems also to emerge in a couple of further differences. It appears, for instance, that within the past three years the members had borrowed more from sources other than INDAP than had the non-members (10% as against 2%) whereas they are the ones best able to profit from INDAP funds. The members thus were more likely to apply for loans anyway. It also appears that many more members than non-members had already joined the committees set up by INDAP

Table 20. Membership of co-operatives and relative deprivation
with regard to income (%)

	Wish to earn more compared with present income:			
	0–50%	50–100%	more than 100%	N
Members	27	31	42	176
Non-members	19	24	57	90
Total	24	29	47	266

χ^2 (2 d.f.) = 5.23

before the coming of the co-operatives (58% v. 22%). Membership of these demanded no financial sacrifice at all, one had merely to apply. To some extent the members displayed the characteristics commonly encountered among the more well-to-do peasants although they hardly differed in status from the non-members.

Also, although the objective results of two of the three co-operatives involved in the survey were hardly phenomenal, the members were more inclined than the non-members to believe that their co-operative had already achieved a considerable degree of success (77% as against 55%). Here, however, I should like to refer once again to a phenomenon which will later prove important when we are discussing solidarity. This is namely that the optimism which influences peasant affiliation is ultimately focused upon a specific goal, the progress and improvement of one's own, privately-owned farm. In 1970 at least, becoming a member of a co-operative did not imply accepting, or holding egalitarian values, or class solidarity.

However, before dealing with this question we must first consider how far membership is linked with the more traditional form of solidarity which we have termed the attraction of the interaction with other peasants from the same community. As indicators for any such link we have taken the overlapping between relationships with family and friends on the one hand, and membership on the other. Tables 21 and 22 clearly show that the data confirm the hypotheses.

The friends and blood relatives of members tend to be members themselves, while those of non-members frequently are not. No obstacle is placed in the way of a friend or

Table 21. Friendship and membership of co-operatives in %

| | Friends | | | |
	are both members	one is a member	neither is a member	N
Members	44	34	22	165
Non-members	16	39	44	79
Total	35	36	30	244

χ^2 (2 d.f.) = 20.42

Table 22. Family relationship and membership of co-operatives in %

| | Relatives are | | | |
	all members	some members	none members	N
Members	27	50	23	120
Non-members	3	43	54	67
Total	18	48	34	187

χ^2 (2 d.f.) = 25.28

relative becoming a member, but it does seem that membership is discussed beforehand within the circle of family or friends. A certain consensus is thus frequently arrived at concerning the desirability of affiliation.

There is no difference at all between members and non-members in the frequency of their affective relationships with friends or with ritual co-parents (84.5% as against 83.6% supplied the names of two friends; 69% as against 69.5% said that they had compadres in the community).

When we examine the frequency of interaction as well, scarcely any difference emerges: 64% of the members, as against 57% of the non-members talk to an estimated four or more other peasants from the community during a normal working day. Hypothesis 4.3 remains unproven. It cannot be said that non-members are more isolated within the community insofar as the *frequency* of their interaction is concerned. It may, however, be true of their *identification* with the community. The members are more inclined to think that their community differs from others in being more friendly (51% v. 34%). Of the members 11% and 25% of non-members think that there is less friendship than in other communities. Another pointer in the same direction may be that the non-members state more frequently (20% as against 10% of members) that they would not know whom to approach for a loan of 300 escudos. This would appear to confirm Hypothesis 4.4 concerning the degree of identification with the local community. The feeling of having ties with family, friends and in some cases certain other members of the community, played a role in affiliation. The question is, whether these ties are also accompanied by feelings of solidarity or by socialising experiences of a more universalistic nature.

In any case any eventual difference in identification with non-related social equals is not the result of a greater degree of religious feeling among the members. In this connection I put a projective question to the respondents concerning 'the majority of the people in the community'. If there is any difference the members are less inclined than the non-members (65% compared with 75%) to think that religion is an important part of life for this majority. There was no evidence either that co-operative members had formed one of an intimate group of friends more often than non-members (59% against 54%) nor are they much more likely to have an intimate friend outside the family (46% as against 40%).

When asked to arrange a number of groups and categories according to the strength of the tie they felt with them, both members and non-members classified the four groups mentioned – family, other relatives, the community and the 'peasants' – in about the same order. Although the slight differences which do exist point in the anticipated direction, the hypothesis remains unproven.

The members do appear to render the traditional mutual aid (vuelta de mano) to other peasants more frequently (41% as against 35% do it every year), but the difference is not large enough for this hypothesis to be regarded as proved[5].

What emerges now from this second series of hypotheses? We have seen that the pros and cons of affiliation are discussed in the circle of primary relations. A certain consensus is arrived at and as it were a common decision taken on whether to join or not. Furthermore, it seems that members identify slightly more with the community. It cannot be said with certainty of co-operative members, as it could of members of the syndicates, that

84

they were more socialized in their intercourse with non-related social peers.

Solidarity may be based both on identification with a community to which one belongs and upon identification with a category of people with whom one has certain interests in common: the small peassant-farmers who find themselves in the same situation. In such a case the members of a co-operative may be expected to show more insight than non-members into the necessity of co-operation for small peasant-farmers.

In actual fact, when asked to suggest solutions for Chile's agrarian problems, the members tended much more than the non-members to propose co-operation among small peasants and forming communal enterprises (50% as against 26%). Another remarkable fact is that, in the other categories of replies to this open question, it is the non-members who most frequently plump for land expropriation (17% as against 5% of the members). According to them, though, this requisitioning would be followed by a redistribution of the land among individual peasants rather than by the setting up of communal farms. Hypothesis 6.1 appears proved.

However, more insight into the need for co-operation does not necessarily mean more action. Asked whether they would accept an offer by nine other peasants to join in a communal enterprise on good land, 71% of the members and 66% of the non-members replied that they would. The most important reason, for members as well as non-members, was that they would then earn more but this reason was relatively more important for the members than for the non-members (39% against 29%). There was no difference between members and non-members when asked if they would then be prepared to sell the land they now owned: 61% as against 59% declared themselves ready to do so.

When asked which they would prefer to earn, 900 escudos on their own little farm or 1500 escudos as members of a communal farm, the non-members were slightly more inclined to prefer the former, as is shown in Table 23. The differences, however, are slight. All in all Hypothesis 6.2 must also be regarded as probable but not proved. The members are not that much more prepared to embark upon a communal project than the non-members. It does seem, however, that if the economic incentive is high, the majority of peasants are prepared to give up their independence, whether they be members or not. On this basis we shall later assert that it is a specific motive – a higher income – which persuades peasants to accept a new value – the communal farm. To what extent do the implications of this new value – equality among peasants, responsibility for other peasants – exist independently of the financial motive just mentioned? When asked which of two

Table 23. Preference with regard to future methods of production in %

	Prefers 900 escudos on own farm	Doesn't know	Prefers 1500 escudos as member of communal farm	N
Members	34	10	56	182
Non-members	45	7	49	92
Total	37	9	54	274

χ^2 (2 d.f.) = 3.61

conflicting statements they agreed with, 11% of the members and 3% of the non-members replied that the highest obligation of a peasant was that towards other peasants. (The others considered their highest obligation to be towards their families.) There are thus a few peasants who have a considerable feeling of solidarity with other peasants and by far the most of these (20 of the 23) are members of co-operatives. This difference may, however, reflect their greater identification with the community, mentioned earlier rather than the much more abstract identification with class.

Asked whether they would accept criticism at a meeting 62% of the members and 51% of the non-members replied that they would. Hypothesis 6.3 is perhaps not entirely proved, but it remains very probable.

Strangely enough it is the members rather than the non-members (9% as against 3%) who think that one peasant progresses at the expense of others. Though only a small number believe this, the hypothesis that the members are less influenced by the Image of the Limited Good, is incorrect. While this Image itself does not (any longer) play a role among 94% of the peasants its absence indicates no enthusiasm for joining a co-operative.

6.3.4   Local differences

It is remarkable how often a hypothesis could not be confirmed, although the data indicated differences between members and non-members in the direction predicted. What is the reason for this? It appears on closer examination that many variables correlated with affiliation in only one or two of the three places involved in the survey. Only two variables clearly had a role to play in all three places: having been a member of the local INDAP committee, and the view taken of land reform, members being more inclined to see a solution in co-operation among peasants. In two places 7 variables correlated with affiliation, and 12 did so in only one place.

In Puente Alto, the most urban farming area, only a couple of other variables were of any importance alongside the two which played a role everywhere. The members believed more strongly in the peasants' future possibilities and they also had a somewhat higher income. In addition, however, they were also clearly less isolated than the non-members: they had more contact with other peasants, had more frequently been one of a group of friends and were thus more socialized. They were also more likely to think that their community, in comparison with others, was a friendlier place to live. In Cuncumen and Lo Abarca too, the most rural places covered by the survey, the non-member was much more isolated than the member. The members more often maintained that their community was characterized by a greater degree of friendship; friendship and kinship relations coincided with membership. And yet it can hardly be assumed that we are dealing here with the same sort of isolation as in Puente Alto. There the isolation of the non-member was that of urban man who scarcely knows his neighbours, has no friends and whose relations with the people he meets are formal, contractual. In Cuncumen and Lo Abarca everyone knows everybody else; the isolation of the non-member does not proceed from the Gesellschaft – characteristics of the community, but from mistrust, suspicion, a fear of being put upon. The non-members state more often than the members (29% v. 9%) that they would not know whom to borrow money from and are less likely (8% as against 21%) to mention a compadre or a relative in this connection. The

Table 24. Multiple correlation of a number of explanatory variables and membership of co-operatives. R^2 is cumulating squared correlation coefficient

Variable	R^2	Fraction explained	Partial correlation coefficient
Entire population (N = 256)			
(53) Previously member of the local committee	0.11	0.07	0.28
(23) Belief in peasants' progress	0.14	0.04	0.23
(69) Belief in success of co-operative	0.19	0.02	0.18
(70) Friends also members	0.22	0.01	0.16
(24) Co-operative view of problems facing agriculture	0.23	0.01	0.14
(50) Identification with community	0.25	0.01	0.14
(72) Relatives also members	0.26	0.01	0.11
Auquinco and Quinahue (N = 77)			
(53) Previously member of the local committee	0.21	0.18	0.49
(29) Prefers lower income on individual plot	0.30	0.10	−0.39
(79) Workers have other interests	0.34	0.04	0.24
(23) Belief in peasants' progress	0.37	0.03	0.20
(14) Credit from source other than INDAP	0.40	0.03	0.21
Concumen and Lo Abarca (N = 140)			
(53) Previously member of local committee	0.11	0.07	0.32
(70) Friends also members	0.20	0.05	0.27
(51) Has somebody to borrow money from	0.27	0.04	−0.26
(69) Positive view of co-operative	0.30	0.02	0.18
(76) Sensitivity to opinion of peers	0.33	0.02	0.19
(72) Relatives also members	0.34	0.02	0.18
(23) Belief in peasants' progress	0.36	0.02	0.16
(78) Image of Limited Good	0.38	0.01	0.13
Puente Alto (N = 35)			
(50) Identification with community	0.26	0.17	0.53
(24) Co-operative view of problems facing agriculture	0.49	0.13	0.48
(23) Belief in peasants' progress	0.52	0.06	0.34
(53) Previously member of local committee	0.56	0.05	0.31

members are more sensitive to the opinion of social equals (64 % as against 41 % are willing to accept criticism). It is as though the members, more than the non-members, are able to use their personal relationships with other people as a basis for new forms of co-operation.

In Auquinco and Quinahue, places which are more developed than Cuncumen, but less urban than Puente Alto, the difference between members and non-members appears to lie more in the non-members' preference for retaining their own family farm; 48 % of them (as against 22 % of the members) would rather earn 900 escudos on their own farm than 1500 escudos on a communal enterprise. The members seem to be more modern in their approach: they read better and more often received credit from a source other than INDAP. The members' insight appears to be based chiefly upon economic considerations. They are less given to mutual aid (35% against 49%) and are more inclined to believe that small peasant farmers and agricultural workers do not share the same interests. Although, more often than the non-members, they had only worked five years in the place (24% as against 7%) they had more experience in participating in a group of friends. This meant that they were more socialized in maintaining friendly relationships with people not related to them.

If, as did INDAP, one sets up co-operatives in places which differ considerably in their level of development and external circumstances, it does not appear that in all cases a certain type of personality will become a member while another type will not. Alongside a certain modern business mentality and the desire to achieve a higher income, one of the most important factors seems to be the degree of confidence which the peasants have in each other. However, in a traditional community, this confidence seems to be based on different qualities in the person who trusts than in a more modern suburban community.

In the light of these differences it is not surprising that a multiple correlation calculation explains only 26% of the variance of membership in the population. As shown in Table 24 this percentage is higher, around 40%, in each of the three communities taken separately, but we are dealing then with smaller numbers of respondents and less divergent observation results.

Nonetheless, the multiple correlation calculation seems to confirm the picture of the member as we had outlined it for the three places. The variable 'previously member of local committee' which plays a role in every case does not, admittedly, tell us anything about the member's personality. It does, however, indicate that it was an inspired move first to unite the peasants in an association like this, which demanded no sacrifice but time and only later to encourage them to join a 'real' co-operative which required some financial sacrifice. While participating in the committee many of the peasants evidently became convinced that INDAP did indeed grant credit, and that it was worth the trouble to continue to receive this even if it meant joining a co-operative. Other traits which characterize the member are a certain optimism with regard to what the future holds for peasants and involvement in the community. In some cases a co-operative mentality is important, while in others it is not. In the last case (Auquinco and Quinahue) a strong determination to improve one's individual, economic lot would seem to provide a substitute.

Notes

1 I derived these two indicators from a study by Bonilla and Silva Michelena who had found a similar difference between members and non-members of rural syndicates in Venezuela (1967, p. 151–2).

2 They can be shown and reproduced on application to the author, Institute of Cultural and Social Studies, State University, Stationsplein 10, Leiden, The Netherlands.

3 I am groping in the dark regarding the average frequency of this phenomenon in Chile. On the fundos which I had not selected with the aim of discovering such ex-members among the respondents, roughly 20% of the members proved to have relinquished their membership.

4 One might imagine that having friends who are also members is the *result* of affiliation. In that case, the dependent variable would be explained with a variable which follows upon it. This idea seems to me incorrect, especially since a similar phenomenon occurs with regard to relatives, as Table 14 showed. If we omit the variable 'affiliation of friends' the remaining variables (together with one other which refers to the year in which the respondents started work in the fundo) still explain 47% of the variation in affiliation.

5 In any case one may conclude that traditional forms of co-operation do not automatically dispose towards joining a co-operative. The difference between the number of members and non-members who *never* practice vuelta de mano is very small; 44 % as against 46 %.

Chapter 7 Leadership and participation

7.1 The functions of leaders

While I did not particularly concern myself with the question of leadership during my research in Chile, it might still be useful, after first dealing with the theory of leadership, to set down what we actually did find out about leaders. During the anthropological part of my research I was made strongly aware of just how important the leadership factor was. Of course it will only be possible to test some of the expectations which we hold on the basis of theory and qualitative research against quantitative data. On the other hand this will help us gain a clearer picture of the problems attaching to the leadership of peasant associations of the sort occurring in Chile.

Sociology tends to take a different view of leadership from that previously held. Formerly the assumption was that it was, so to speak, a person's irresistible leadership qualities which led to him becoming a leader. At the present time, however, there is a clearer realization that, in the last instance, it is the expectation of the *group members* that the leader will make a positive contribution towards satisfying their needs which makes them accept leadership at all.

A large number of investigations into leadership have shown that the leader has two main functions, one *instrumental* and one *expressive*. The instrumental function relates to the leader's contribution towards achieving the aims of the group (or organization), while his expressive function has to do with his contribution towards preserving its essential unity. In some organizations each of these functions may be fulfilled by a different leading individual, although one leader can also take care of both (cf. Etzioni, 1969).

Both leadership functions appear necessary in the Chilean peasant organizations which we studied. Syndicate leaders must be able to bring about and maintain the unity of the organization and at the same time be capable of formulating objectives, establishing a policy, carrying on negotiations, and advancing cogent arguments for their standpoint. They must be able to build up relationships with politicians and high-ranking officials with a view to winning them over in case of conflict. They must be able to envisage an acceptable future agrarian structure. Leaders of co-operatives too, albeit in different spheres of activity, must be able to forecast possible developments. They too must be capable of establishing relationships and of negotiating with government agencies. In addition they must possess a considerable business instinct. The economic activities initiated by the co-operative must show a profit and new profitable activities must constantly be embarked upon. This requires not only a good choice of activities, but also involves entering into contracts with third parties and keeping them, administering and making the best possible use of one's own and borrowed money and ensuring that the members in their turn fulfil their obligations towards the co-operative. The co-operative leader must

90

also preserve the unity of the members.

Accordingly, as an outsider, the researcher establishes that the Chilean peasant leaders must indeed fulfil the two functions mentioned. He also notes in passing, however, that in the vast majority of syndicates and co-operatives with which he became acquainted, both the actual organization and the way it was run were imposed from outside. The fact that leaders existed did not necessarily follow from the requirements and expectations of the members, but could also result from the imposed obligation to elect a board. I remember being present at a couple of board elections where voters had no very clear idea of what they were doing in the first place and were particularly ignorant of what function, the instrumental or the expressive, the person elected would have to fulfil. 'He's a very nice chap, but he's hopeless at taking decisions', I was told of the newly elected chairman of one local committee of a regional co-operative. During another election, in a small production group, the older members chose an instrumental leader while the younger voted for an expressive one. Neither faction, however, was clearly aware of the reason for its choice.

Although one person was not always necessarily incapable of fulfilling the two leadership functions in a reasonable manner, most elected leaders could be called more instrumental than expressive, or vice versa. The ignorance of practically all those involved with these two functions caused leaders to be criticized for not being precisely what they were not. The expressive leader, the man who wanted no quarrel with anyone, but who was also very short on initiative, was reproached for lack of vision, for not being a man of action. Of the instrumental leader it was said that he would not allow others their say, was incapable of delegating, took charge of everything himself.

Although it may not be a simple matter to explain that leaders have to fulfil two functions and that it may pay to choose a different person for each function, it seems to me most essential that the peasants should be made aware of this.

The Chilean context itself created yet another function for the peasant leaders to fulfil: the *ideological*. The peasants had to be taught to embrace the ideals relating to a much more collectively organized production structure such as was advocated both in some INDAP, CORA and PDC circles and in the opposition parties on the left. This involved making them aware of their situation and broadening and deepening certain values such as equality and participation. Initially this was the task of government employees and ideologically trained party members, but after that it devolved upon the convinced peasants themselves. To a greater or lesser degree INDAP, CORA and the political parties canvassing the countryside all wanted those peasants who shared their ideals elected as administrators. Various pressures were exercised at meetings in order to get the desired people elected. Thus it came about that peasant leaders were more or less expected to propagate certain values and norms among the members. I received the definite impression during my participation at meetings that those leaders who really lived out these particular values and norms managed to get them accepted by the members. Those who only gave lip service to them, failed to convince.

7.2 The dysfunctions of leadership

The Chilean context played a role in yet another respect. In social structures where patronage is an important mechanism, there is a tendency to regard public or otherwise collective resources over which one has the disposal as a means of enhancing one's own status. Such a tendency is not infrequently found among those holding government posts or those who are in a position to take decisions or influence the allocation of public funds. People who have connections with higher officials who control the allocation of means, may, in exchange for a consideration or a reciprocal service, use these connections, as intermediaries or 'brokers', to bring others into contact with these officials. A place on the board of a co-operative or syndicate is a key position which carries with it special connections and sometimes control over public funds. These connections may spring from the relationships maintained by board members, agricultural and local government agencies and officials. I am referring to the agencies dealing with land reform, agricultural credit and extension and the judiciary and administrative authorities which decide on the outcome of workers' conflicts and so forth. Board members may become involved in the allocation of financial resources when decisions concerning the granting of credit and the setting up of certain development projects are, to some extent, left to the local community.

Those who set up the peasant organizations never intended leadership positions to be used for self advantage by means of patronage or 'brokerage'. They cherished the hope that the organization might help to raise the status of all its members. Moreover they expected the organization to be democratic in the sense that all members would have an equal say in matters concerning the organization and exercise such control over board members that the latter could not abuse their positions.

However, as Landsberger & Hewitt (1970) correctly point out, turning a leadership position to one's own advantage is one of the alternatives open to the peasant who hopes to enhance his individual status. Since, as we saw in the previous chapter, one of the most important affiliation motives of the Chilean peasant is precisely the hope of improving his own lot it is to be expected that in some cases at least leadership will thus be abused. Such abuse is dysfunctional, not because it confounds the expectations of the government or of political ideologists, but because it makes the members suspicious of their leaders, confirms a familiar and traditional pattern of behaviour and hinders acceptance by the members of 'new' values such as equality and participation.

Apart from a few isolated cases I found no indication that peasant leaders abused their positions. What I did find, especially in the co-operatives (in the syndical movement this only held good for leaders on a provincial or national level), was a lively conviction among the members, sometimes accompanied by veiled accusations, that a particular administrator was feathering his own nest. The only quantitative datum at my disposal is the finding that relatively more leaders than members of co-operatives had received credit from INDAP and other sources. This could mean that they had taken advantage of their closer relationship with INDAP officials, but it is also a commonly found phenomenon that more modern farmers receive more credit. The pejorative interpretation, thus, need not necessarily be correct. It seems to me that the sequence of events was as follows: the more modern peasant farmers had a greater need of the services which INDAP could provide. Since INDAP preferred to provide these services by way of committees and, later, co-operatives, it was precisely these peasants who worked hard to get such associations off the ground. Having shown such enthusiasm they were elected members of the board and since their need for credit was greatest they were the first to apply for it.

Only when their application has been successful and when, in addition, credit becomes scarcer because there are more people soliciting it, does the suspicion arise that the leader has been favouring himself.

Suspicions appeared to occur more frequently than the facts might warrant, although admittedly it is difficult for an outsider who is only spending a short time in a community, to be sure of what actually happened. One Board member was said to have illegally appropriated a quantity of wooden stakes, another was accused of using the lorry too much for his own private business, a third of selling his tractor to the co-operative at too high a price. A fourth was reproached with wanting to become a manager and so receive a salary from the co-operative, a fifth (and sixth and seventh) was accused of fiddling the expenses for a trip to Santiago, an eighth was said to owe his candidature to being a member of Party X while a ninth was held to have been ordered by his party, Y, to ensure the failure of the co-operative. . . .

Only scrupulous behaviour, it would seem, backed up by documentary proof and subject to regular institutional control, would prevent such allegations. However, the inability of both leaders and members to receive and hand out criticism as role-bearers instead of as individuals and the usually deficient manner in which the books were kept, led one to fear that, for the time being at last, this would remain a pious hope.

In the following chapter I shall argue that this suspicion on the part of the members, whether justified or not, prevents them from acknowledging the solidarity of those leaders they mistrust. This is detrimental to his solidarity in the end. I might also refer here to another dysfunctional result: the suspect leader is no longer a shining example, he does not encourage people to accept those values which he puts into practice.

7.3 The differences between leaders and members of syndicates

We have considered as leaders all those who at the time of the survey occupied or had occupied an administrative position in the committee on the estate or in the syndicate. Since we did not draw up any explicit hypotheses concerning the differences between leaders and members, we shall regard the results merely as pointers. Although we did not either operationalize in advance any variables to determine the extent to which the leadership was instrumental, expressive or ideological, the differences may be largely contained under these denominators.

Just as in previous chapters a difference is regarded as real when the chi-square value surpasses that which corresponds with the 5 % level of significance.

So far as their *instrumental* function is concerned, leaders seem to have a somewhat higher status on the fundo than do the members; they are more likely to be inquilinos (49 % as against 33 %). Leaders have a higher standard of education and are better at reading. They joined the syndicate earlier than the members and more frequently received a training course from INDAP. They did not, as I had expected on the basis of Affonso *et al.* (1970), prove to have worked more often outside agriculture.

It is noteworthy that, despite their somewhat higher status, the leaders earn less than the members. This probably explains why they feel a greater relative deprivation.

Their *expressive* function seems to emerge in the fact that the leaders are more likely to have lived and worked on the fundo from before 1950. They more frequently have compadres than the members (80 % against 56 %) and those leaders who have compadres, also have more of them. Although they do not tend much more often to have an intimate

Table 25. Leadership and patronage in syndicates (in %)

	Patronage index				N
	1 (low)	2	3	4 (high)	
Leaders	15	34	34	17	41
Ordinary members	4	19	47	30	102

χ^2 (3 d.f.) = 10.9

friend (56% as against 51%) nor to have formed part of a group of friends (63% as against 56%) the leaders do believe more readily than the members that there is more friendship in their fundo than in others (56% as against 27%).

Both *instrumental* and *ideological* functions are served by the fact that the leaders score lower than the members on the patronage index, as Table 25 shows. In itself this lower score is not so surprising, but it becomes so when we remember our earlier finding that, compared with the member, the non-member had a higher patronage score, had come to work on the fundo earlier and had more people financially dependent on him. The leaders also came to work earlier on the fundo than did the members, they too have more people under their roof who are financially dependent on them (51% of the leaders as against 22% of the members have four or more such people at home) but with them these variables have not led to a higher patronage score, as they did with the non-members.

Precisely because, in some respects, leaders resemble non-members more than they do members, it is improbable that their lower score on the patronage index is a consequence of their leadership. A more likely explanation is that they are people who, despite their dependence, turned their backs on the owner, felt more deprived than others, and joined the syndicate at an early stage.

Also functional from the *ideological* viewpoint is the fact that the leaders, in comparison with the members, are somewhat readier to work their regalias on a communal basis (70% as against 60%). They are also more likely than the members to mention the asentamiento as their second choice for a desired agrarian future, after their own little piece of land (44% as against 18%). In addition they place the working class higher on the list of groups with which they feel a tie (4.75 against 5.61).

Just as remarkable as the differences are the similarities between leaders and members on the instrumental and ideological plane. They take the same view of the syndicate's task, give the same answer to the question of whether the syndicate pays sufficient attention to what happens on their fundo and have the same opinion of what land reform should entail.

The material seems to indicate that syndicate leaders are people whose most important instrumental quality is their aversion to the patron and who are in the main informal, expressive leaders, in the sense of stars in a sociogram.

7.4 The differences between leaders and members of co-operatives

In dealing with the co-operatives we have again regarded as leaders those who occupied or had occupied an administrative function in the local committees or in the co-operative at the time of the survey. Although we did not formulate any hypotheses regarding these leaders either, the differences with the members may once again be classified under the headings: instrumental, expressive and ideological functions. Here too the results must be regarded merely as indications.

The board members of co-operatives are able to exercise their *instrumental function* because they are more modern in their farming methods. They differ from the members in a number of variables which are familiar from adoption–diffusion studies. The leaders have a higher standard of education than the members, are better skilled at reading, received credit (both input and capital credit) more often from INDAP as well as from other sources, were more likely to keep accounts and visited a large city more frequently. Admittedly the leaders' farms are no bigger, but they do have a somewhat higher income than the members. They also aspire to a higher income and more often contract paid workers on their farms. They are more likely than the members to be employers. In the light of this it no longer seems strange that the leaders, as I was frequently informed during the exploratory stage of the investigation, are inclined to have the co-operative undertake precisely those tasks which suit their own more modern farming methods.

Nonetheless, it seems that the leaders also fulfil an *expressive function*. They tend more often than the members to have an intimate friend and were, more frequently, one of a group of friends. By and large they conversed with more colleagues during the week. They were rated higher on a solidarity index. In comparison with the ordinary members, the leaders are also more inclined to make excuses for those peasants who have not yet joined the co-operative. The leaders, however, are not remarkably different from the *ideological* viewpoint. They are more inclined than the members to prefer a higher income on a communal farm to a lower income on a farm of their own, and tend more to think that small peasant-farmers and farm workers share the same interests. It is worth noting that leaders appear to differ from members in ways in which we had originally expected members would differ from non-members.

7.5 Participation an oligarchization

Even before 1960 the ideal of participation was alive in Chile in certain circles of the PDC and the parties on the left. This ideal implied that decision making in peasant organizations should proceed democratically, and involve all the members. They would then work together to implement these decisions. Although the ideal usually remained vague, a number of peasants and officials of INDAP and CORA nonetheless realized that participation must also imply the regular rotation of board members. The tendency of leaders to cling on to their leadership, their inclination towards oligarchization, would have to be fought and overcome.

I do not doubt that this tendency existed, even though I have no quantitative data to confirm this supposition. It was not, however, always deliberate policy on the part of the leaders themselves. In some cases where for example election to some office meant considerable material advantage, or a great increase in prestige, there may indeed have been an inclination to cling to this status, once achieved. If often happened, however, that people at the head of an active association who had learned their role while actually on the job, built up such a considerable advance in expertise, in organizatory skill and in the size of their networks during their term in office that in fact they had to be re-elected if the organization was not to slip back.

The long continuance in office noted by de Ranitz and de Ranitz (1972, p. 128) in three asentamientos, does not seem to me exceptional. It is known that worker self government runs the risk of failure due to the oligarchization of the leaders. No particular effort was made in Chilean peasant organizations to build up an administrative structure which might counteract this tendency. Control commissions in co-operatives and asentamientos – which had in any case been adapted from foreign models – worked badly or not at all. Neither the government nor any other specialized institutes paid much attention to the problem of oligarchization. People seemed to pin their hopes on a regular rotation of individuals occupying leadership functions, and on the leader's preparedness to make way for others. Such hopes appear somewhat naive, assuming as they do a considerable degree of self denial and solidarity in people who have cause to value their own personal share in the development of the organization more highly than that of others.

From the theoretical point of view these hopes have implications which were not always realized in Chile. If we assume that leaders are chosen by groups because they are able to make a contribution which is valued by the members, then this implies that such a contribution is chiefly expected from particular persons. Their leadership depends on the one hand upon the group but on the other upon their personal qualities. This is seen very clearly in the case of informal leaders who only gain recognition if they have a valuable contribution to give. Not everyone is an informal leader and it is not easy to set oneself up as one. If someone who started out as an informal leader is appointed to an administrative post he cannot be replaced by just anybody, but only by another informal leader who fulfils the same function. The main thing then is to train members in such a way that the group acknowledges them as informal leaders.

As the expertise of the first leader increases, he becomes more difficult to replace. For the time being the talent necessary to provide competent leadership for production or service co-operatives appears so thin on the ground that my hopes of easy replacement are not very high.

There is the additional factor that, if he is replaced and certainly if he takes this to heart, the board member remains an informal leader and his resentment may cause him to stir up his followers against his replacement. If somebody is elected to the Board simply because a vacancy exists, then he is indeed much easier to replace, but he is also ineffective as a leader.

In short, our argument amounts to this. If the ideal of participation is to have any chance of success then administrative structures must be developed in which authority is circumscribed and subject to control. Furthermore ways must be found to provide the members in general and those with leadership qualities in particular with the information necessary for them to play their part in decision making and to develop their talents. If leaders are, in addition, required to be politically reliable (by the government or the opposition parties) their replacement becomes all the more difficult.

It will be obvious from all this that I am sceptical about the possibility of a regular rotation of leaders. It will also appear that I place more hopes in the devising of a structure which would allow for free control and criticism. Yet this too has its difficulties. I was often struck during meetings by the fact that the peasants criticized – and were criticized – as individuals and not as role bearers. The diffuse, fairly complicated relationship existing between any two peasants in a small community makes it more difficult for them to absorb the fact that criticism of a leader affects only one of the roles in their relationship. The result is that the leader – who is also a compadre, or the friend of a friend, or the fellow one does a few days work for during the harvest season – will react to criticism as to a hostile act. Since the critic knows this he will not offer his criticism openly, during a meeting, but mutter slanderously beforehand. In this way the criticism, or the rumour, becomes a weapon in the struggle between factions, or an incitement to the emergence of factions. The critic finds supporters, but the leader, feeling ill-used, calls upon his relatives and friends to protect him. Such a state of affairs can lead to a complete absence of control or criticism, and this happens in many co-operatives where the official control commission does not function. Yet, on the other hand, control or criticism may indeed lead to the formation of factions.

The only solution I can see, is to make an effort, using socio-dramas, for instance, to teach both leaders and members that they are role-bearers, and that it is possible to separate both cognitive and affective roles. This of course is more important for the leaders. Once they show that they are not afraid of criticism and do not consider it a hostile act, the members will soon make themselves heard.

Chapter 8 Co-operation and solidarity

8.1 Introduction

One of the most important questions which remains to be answered concerns the viability and effectiveness of the new co-operative associations and enterprises of the Chilean peasants. This viability of course depends in part upon societal factors and processes, and mainly upon the government and its specialized agencies. Here, however, we shall confine ourselves to asking which factors, on the individual and group level of the participating peasants, determine the viability of these organizations.

In more concrete terms, this poses the following questions:
– How ought the Chilean peasants to behave in order to make a success of the co-operative associations and enterprises in which they participate?
– Are we indeed justified in expecting such behaviour of peasants, or is it more probable that they will behave differently?
– If the latter is true, how is this behaviour to be changed?

The answer to the first question appears simple. Peasants will achieve successful forms of co-operation – insofar at least as this depends on them and not upon the prevailing social structure – if they properly fulfil certain roles, that is to say, satisfy the norms pertaining to these roles. But will they do this? And why should they? Simply because they realize that this is in their own best interests? It seems to me that this is not sufficient. The realization that a certain form of behaviour is in their own interests is a necessary condition, but not a sufficient one. In order to make this clear we shall have to retrace our steps. What do we really mean by co-operation? What does a co-operating peasant do? He carries out to the letter any task entrusted to him, pays his dues, attends meetings, observes the working hours, does not grow rich at the organization's expense, keeps abreast of the organization's problems and helps to solve them, and abides by decisions legitimately arrived at. In a word, he keeps the rules, among the most important of which is the rule which decides how conflicts or differences of opinion must be overcome. Two conclusions may be drawn from all this:
– Not every act is one of co-operation. A peasant working his own land is not engaged in co-operation, yet is serving his own interest.
– Insofar as co-operation implies an action (and not refraining from an action) it consists of utilizing his resources, which are: affection, energy, knowledge, time and money. Insofar as co-operation consists of refraining from an action, it implies relinquishing satisfactions which might perhaps have been enjoyed in another, non-legitimate manner.

Retracing our steps has already brought one problem to light. Co-operation is frequently not the only kind of action which serves the individual, material interest of the peasant. We shall have to discover what this self interest consists of exactly. A second problem remained rather more implicit – do all these various co-operative actions really serve the peasant's self interest so directly? The example we have given in which co-operation also implied refraining from some action which, on the face of it, would seem to serve the peasant's own interest, reveals that this is not always to. The question becomes all the more interesting when we reflect that, in a newly founded peasant organization, there are as yet no internalized norms to govern these actions nor are there any members who know exactly what is expected of them according to the statutes. This being so, is it probable that the members will act co-operatively, solely because they see it as in their own interest? Should there not, in addition, be other motives to guide the peasants' conduct? In our opinion there are. *Coercion* and *solidarity* may exist as motives alongside *utilitarian* considerations. We shall discuss solidarity in a second theoretical digression, but first we must probe more deeply into the problem of interest.

8.2 Peasant interests and conflicts of interest

We shall define interest as the possibility of obtaining income or other forms of satisfaction. This possibility is chiefly determined by a person's position in the production process. For peasants participating in a co-operative venture it frequently happens that not all those actions which serve their own interests are also co-operative actions. The participant in a collective farm nearly always possesses a piece of land for his own use. If a peasant has to divide his resources between actions which serve his interest directly and those which do so only via a detour, this can give rise to tension, the same tension that affects anyone who has to choose between immediate and delayed need gratification. Economic theory assumes that direct gratification will generally be given preference. This implies that people can only be persuaded to postpone satisfaction of their own needs by being offered some extra reward. At the same time it must be remembered that newly instituted co-operatives or collective farms (and, to a lesser extent, syndicates), while promising to be of material advantage to the members, still have to make good this promise. This means that, particularly in the initial period, motives other than self interest are heavily drawn upon.

There is, however, another factor. Olson (1965) has shown that a person – assuming that he will try to obtain the maximum possible benefit – will not be inclined to exert himself to acquire collective goods if he will also acquire them without effort.

The result or yield of a co-operative venture in agriculture is to a certain extent equivalent to a collective good in Olson's sense of the word. In this respect agriculture differs from industry. The wage improvements, gained by the syndicate, also benefit the non-members. The co-operative which opens up a market for a particular product, or breaks the monopoly of a certain buyer by introducing competitors into the area, is providing advantages to non-members as well. All the members share in the good grain harvest enjoyed by a communal farm according to the amount of work they have put into the farm. But such a differential distribution of benefits should also be possible in industry. Why then does the collective product in agriculture bear more resemblance to a collective good? Because in agriculture, without a very careful check, it is impossible to say which specific process is responsible for the end product being inferior in quality or disappointing in quantity. It is impossible to discover just who was careless in his work. Were the fields not ploughed deep enough? Was the seed in fact treated with pesticides? Was somebody careless in weeding? Was the seed delivered not of top quality? Was the rainfall in any particular month too high, or, on the contrary, was the weather too dry? Was the right amount of fertilizer used?

Disappointing results may be attributed to environmental factors outside anyone's control (the weather), to suppliers (who failed to deliver the seed or the fertilizer on time or who delivered inferior quality goods), or to tasks badly performed, that is, to other members who have skimped their work but who cannot be taken to task since it would cost too much to check up on their activities. In other words the multiplicity of factors which may be involved ensures that it is always possible to foist the blame onto other members of the co-operative. Now is it clear that if none of the members of the association worked towards obtaining the product, there would be nothing to obtain. But if a number of members strive to obtain it, then another member has less reason to do so. After all, even if he makes no effort, thus conserving resources with which he may serve his own interests more directly, he still acquires his share of the collective good in the end[1].

An extra incentive is needed to persuade the members to work towards obtaining the collective good. Such an incentive may be material (in the form of extra pay), may be based on coercion, or may be of a normative nature. This last may involve the sacrifice of resources for the benefit of others.

Not only the production, but also the distribution of the product of a co-operative enterprise may give rise to conflicts of interest. Generally speaking this will occur under one of three conditions. The *distribution of power* among the participants may be such that some are able to appropriate more of the end product than others. The *scarcity of a service* a person can provide may make it possible for him to claim a more than equitable share of the proceeds. This might also be regarded as a question of power, but there is a difference. Power can be redistributed, a specialized skill cannot. Finally, the product may prove to be what the economists call *indivisible*, so that some will inevitably receive more than others. If the fruits of a communal effort consist of certain services, indivisibility will of necessity result.

We have so far dealt with the interests of the individual peasant who participates in a co-operative or a collective farm. There are also, however, several remarks to be made concerning the conflict of interests between groups or categories.

The conflict with which we are most familiar from sociological theory is of course that between classes, between those who dispose of the means of production and those who do not. The latter are able to survive only by selling their labour. Without wishing yet to discuss this theory in any depth we must nonetheless point out that it does not sufficiently explain the various actions which peasants take to promote their interests.

While not losing sight of Marx's sound view that such a conflict of interests is built into the organization of production within society, one must also bear in mind that the labour market is not the only market in which such conflicts arise. Precisely in the case of independent peasants who possess their own means of production (and in the case of a collective farm) other markets are at least as important in explaining their conflicting interests and the conduct they adopt. It follows from this that the various categories of peasants do not always share the same interests. Small peasant farmers, for instance, like the landed proprietors, are interested in high prices for their products and low wages. In the first market, that of the producers, they find themselves opposed by the urban consumers, including the urban proletariat, while the agricultural workers may be largely on their side. This is often referred to as the conflict between town and country. In other markets the various categories of the rural population are likely to clash. By relating interest conflicts to different markets which in some cases may in their turn consist of subsidiary markets, we obtain a very complex picture in which nobody any longer has exactly the same interest as anybody else. Interest aggregation then means concentrating on certain common interests and ignoring those which are not shared and which at that particular moment appear less important. This makes class, in Marx's sense, not impossible, but certainly a borderline case.

When thus, within a collectivity, one finds groups which do not occupy exactly the same position in the production process and have thus divergent interests on particular markets or subsidiary markets, sub-collectivities may emerge whose interests to some extent conflict. The action taken by the collectivity itself – in advocating land reform for instance – may also create different positions; agricultural workers who become asentados and those who remain wage labourers on the land.

Interest aggregation is thus a dynamic phenomenon; interest groups may form, co-operate and then break up again. This may happen due to a change in their position in the production process, but it may also come about without any objective alteration in their interests. It is sufficient that they start to view their interest in a different light, attaching less weight to the common interest they stressed earlier and more to those which are not shared.

It will be clear from the foregoing analysis that when peasants decide to co-operate this does not mean that latent conflicts of interest between individuals, families, sub-groups, groups (farms) and sub-collectivities, have disappeared altogether.

We have seen, moreover, that, while it is true that the peasant's self-interest is served by the production of the collective good, this insight alone will not be sufficient to persuade him to exert himself permanently in order to attain that good.

In a later section we shall give examples to show that the tensions referred to did occur in Chilean peasant organizations. We shall accordingly discuss ways of lessening such tensions and safeguarding the functioning of the organizations. First, however, we shall try to discover what other motives may lead an individual to sacrifice some of his resources.

8.3 Solidarity

A peasant can devote his resources to promoting his own interests and to acts of co-operating. These acts serve his interests indirectly, sometimes very indirectly, and may involve the sacrifice of his own resources for the welfare of others. The nature of the collective good which is the product of co-operation is such that co-operative actions nearly always entail such a sacrifice.

It seems to us that there are three motives which may impel a peasant to thus invest his resources. These are *coercion*, the prospect of *reward* and *solidarity*. Compulsion and reward, however, mean that this investment cannot now be regarded as a sacrifice. The peasant who, by co-operating well, avoids exclusion from the group by way of sanction and the peasant who is paid for co-operating are both directly serving their own interests. With what we term solidarity the position is somewhat different.

The definitions given to solidarity in sociological literature vary widely. We would define solidarity as the willingness to sacrifice resources or immediate gratification for the welfare of others, out of a feeling of unity. It means doing something for others without the prospect of material reward.

We make a further distinction between *mechanical* and *organic* solidarity. Mechanical solidarity entails sacrificing resources for a common goal. Organic solidarity is the sacrifice of gratifications in order to preserve the unity of the group.

To establish under what conditions solidarity will emerge and survive we must look at it more closely. We note first of all that a willingness to make sacrifices for others implies that this willingness is confined to *certain particular* others. On this point our definition of solidarity differs from that which Friedrichs (1960, p. 497) gave of altruism: 'the inhibiting or controlling of ego's behaviour to provide for the satisfaction of alter's impulses or desires'. Whereas for Friedrichs altruism is a quality displayed by individuals everywhere and towards everyone, solidarity is a quality of individuals with regard to certain others[2]. In relation to an individual one cannot speak of solidarity in general, but only of his solidarity with a particular group or category. It is quite possible for a person to feel more solidarity with one group than with another of which he is also a member.

There is one important conclusion to be drawn from this, namely that solidarity is a concept to be employed only in relation to a definite group or category. The inherent implication is also important. *It is that groups and collectivities compete for the solidarity of the individual who is a member of both.* This insight is not new, but it has not, perhaps, been sufficiently stressed. When Blau (1964, p. 285) says that 'social solidarity in macrostructures is always problematical, because the particularistic values that unite ingroups create segregating boundaries between them in the higher collectivity', he is referring to conflicting solidarities which are not resolved by the solidarity with an embracing social unit. If social pressure is exercised upon a person's solidarity (i.e. the fact that he makes part of his resources available to the group) by each group (or collectivity) to which he belongs, this will lead to rivalry between them. We are assuming here that:

a. these resources are limited, and that
b. they are always allocated and are not kept 'in reserve'.

Assumption a. may be readily accepted but the position is rather different with assumption b. While acknowledging that most people *have* allocated their resources, some of these allocations are not so important that their re-distribution would provoke immediate protest. This, however, will happen ultimately.

People who belong to many groups and collectivities will try to find some way of accommodating the different claims made upon their resources. This usually works so well in daily life that they are scarcely aware of being pulled in several directions at once. The methods used are based upon the replacement of one resource by another. Time, energy, care or love are usually replaced by money, although other replacements are conceivable. Groups or organizations often employ people whose daily task it is to promote the interests of the group and they are paid for this work.

Competition for solidarity between groups is chiefly evident during mobilization, when a re-allocation of resources takes place, and in those circumstances in which a group or organization lays a permanent, heavy claim upon the resources of the members. The sluggishness which accompanies the mobilization of a collectivity does not spring necessarily from any disagreement about the aims of that collectivity. It is much more likely that members are chary of incurring the reproaches of groups from which resources will have to be withdrawn. The rivalry theory also explains why mobilization seems inevitably to be followed by a period of slackening interest and disenchantment (Van Doorn, 1968, p. 8). The longer a new, one-sided allocation lasts the more the rival groups suffer from it and the greater the insistence upon a new re-allocation, that is, a return to the former allocation.

All this means that mobilization will prove very difficult so long as groups which fulfil an important function in the lives of the members continue to exist alongside the mobilized collectively. And there will be many such groups[3]. In a modern differentiated society, with its emphasis upon the right of the individual to develop whatever gifts he possesses to the full, an individual will belong to many groups. If, then, the pressure upon individuals to preserve the mobilization is kept up, reluctance, disillusionment and passive resistance will continue to grow. It is only possible to achieve a new balance if all rival solidarities are to some extent respected.

Finally, it must be pointed out that, with regard to the emergence of rival solidarities, it makes little difference whether the groups in question impinge upon each other in one individual or whether one group, in it entirety, is swallowed up by another, larger group.

Rivalry will occur in both cases, although in the first instance group links will tend to be more individualized since the combination of groups to which people belong varies from one individual to another. Whereas in the second case there is more question of a collective decision regarding the allocation of resources, in the first the decision is an individual one. Simmel (1969, p. 148–150) has already pointed out that from the historical viewpoint the second form of association is the earliest form of multiple group membership. It 'enables the single individual to participate in a number of groups without alienating him from his affiliation with his original locality'. In this respect our own finding that membership in friendly or kin groups tended not to crosscut affiliation in peasant syndicates or co-operatives is highly significant.

The implications to which we have just referred concerned *mechanical* solidarity, the sacrifice of resources. But is this the kind of solidarity required in a peasant organization, be it a co-operative, a collective farm or an agricultural syndicate? It seems to me that mechanical solidarity, endeavour for the common cause, is especially required during and shortly after the period of mobilization. It must be borne in mind that every newly founded interest organization must of necessity detract from other interests and interest groups. Once the organization is firmly on its feet, there is a tendency to demobilize. A co-operative, for instance, begins to employ people to perform particular tasks and thus ceases to be dependent on the trojan work performed by the members in their spare time. But now, assuming that the organization is functioning and beginning to bear fruit – a distribution problem arises. In addition to a certain mechanical solidarity in the form of contribution or participation, the members are also required to give proof of *organic* solidarity. In other words they are required to refrain from harming the organization by refusing to abide by the distribution of tasks or the allocation of benefits. They must accept the results and the procedures employed in settling differences. The longer an organization exists and grows in complexity, and the larger it is, the more differentiated it must necessarily be. In other words, there will be more specialization of labour and probably more variation in the rates of pay. This will bring about a corresponding need for increased organic solidarity. The units (members or sub-groups) will have to recognize the justice of the exchange relationships in which they are involved.

It is clear that, as this unavoidable differentiation increases, the need for organic solidarity will grow. But at the same time there is an increasing probability that those who consider themselves, for whatever reason, badly done by in the distribution, will join together (mobilization, mechanical solidarity) to improve their position. The organization, the social system in which this occurs, can survive, and find a new key to distribution just so long as the quarrel is thrashed out within the framework established by the rules. If this framework is breached – if fights break out or a group decides to quit – then the system may cease to be viable. Thus, a functioning social system characterized by differentiation has two main requirements – a certain degree of mechanical solidarity and a fairly large measure of organic solidarity. Neither of these can be taken for granted; they can grow or they can decline. Both are threatened by the mechanical solidarity of sub-groups.

Socialist societies, at least in the past, tended to seek to solve this problem of balance by denying this differentiation, by centralizing decisions rather than by evolving processes of deliberation and compromise firmly anchored in the constitution. In other words the accent was laid upon a further extension of the social system with which, it was hoped, the individual felt most solidary. A certain degree of coercion was even resorted to in order to obtain the desired behaviour. These attempts met with little success. The larger the social unit within which mechanical solidarity is required, the more sub-groups there will be with divergent objectives and, in consequence, the more conflicting sub-solidarities. This will make mechanical solidarity more difficult to achieve and it will be all the more important to replace this mechanical solidarity by organic solidarity.

By way of hypothesis we postulate here that in a differentiated social system, a mixture of mechanical and organic solidarity is a functional requirement for development. Members must be willing to strive for common goals and be able to accept a distribution of advantages arrived at on the basis of consultation. We may assume that the distribution of their resources (over system objectives and sub-system objectives) and of gratifications (throughout the sub-systems or units) will only be accepted voluntarily if they are considered just. The idea of what is just is to some extent culturally determined but there is a limit to the ideological manipulation to which it can be subjected. A second hypothesis is that the extent to which a distribution (of resources or gratifications) is considered just, depends upon the degree in which the units participate in the decision making which determines this distribution and thus also upon the extent to which an administration is liable to sanction.

In general, however, the process of consultation and compromise described above as an ideal is not constant but occurs only sporadically. There will be periods in which a particular distribution of tasks and rewards is laid down and comes to be regarded as a norm. Later, this norm will not be subject to continuing consultation and compromise.

In the local communities in which co-operatives and collective farms are set up there are often as yet no norms governing the behaviour to be expected of members of such organizations. The solidarity required of villagers embraces compliance with *existing* norms, and does not take into account all possible or conceivable norms. A modern organization also requires that members observe certain rules governing the division of labour, the distribution of produce and the supervision of the various tasks (see Dore, 1971), rules which either do not exist at all in a traditional society or are differently formulated. It is therefore not as easy to graft a modern co-operative structure upon a tightly knit peasant community as Fals Borda (1970) would seem to suggest. There is the additional factor that traditional solidarity is chiefly mechanical, that is to say, it inhibits the peasants from pursuing their individual interests, which in itself is a condition of agricultural development. Consequently a growth in individualism is often accompanied by a decline in traditional solidarity, a transition 'from brotherhood to otherhood' as Chodak (1972) termed it.

Solidary behaviour, the willingness to make sacrifices for the sake of others, is in the first instance a gift and we know from the anthropological literature (e.g. Mauss, 1967) that a gift creates obligations for the recipient. He must reciprocate in some way. In a very worthwhile article Gouldner (1960) has pointed out that reciprocity appears to be a general human norm, which, moreover, is implicitly assumed in functional theory. If a person displays solidarity with a group this can be very functional for that group, but does not explain why this solidary behaviour persists. The real reason is that the individual displaying solidarity is recompensed. What are the advantages with which other group members can and must reward solidarity? One form of compensation is *reciprocity* in solidary behaviour. This reciprocity assumes that the group in question already recognizes norms governing the behaviour of members of associations. Another form of return consists in giving *prestige* to the solidary individual and, not infrequently, a leadership function as well. This will occur chiefly where norms and roles have not yet been elaborated. Finally, another possibility is failure to recognize the sacrifice. The others will then continue to wonder suspiciously just what selfish gain the solidary individual aspires to.

At this point it seems advisable to recapitulate briefly the most important findings we have made thus far:

– Peasant organizations cannot function solely on the basis of the interest, the material reward of the members. Mechanical solidarity is required in the initial period, and as the differentiation of tasks and rewards within the organization increases so too does the need for organic solidarity.

– Both the mechanical and the organic solidarity of the members with such an organization is impaired by a strong mechanical solidarity within sub-groups.

– The best distribution of rights and obligations is that which is regarded as just and accepted as a norm. Participation by units and sub-groups in decisions affecting this distribution appears to be the best way of achieving this.

– On the other hand an outside answer to the question of what is just and what scope the value of justice ought to have may also be accepted. In this case we are dealing with what may be called growing political awareness. This, however, is a cultural innovation which had not yet been adopted by the majority of Chilean peasants at the time of our research.

– In addition to participation and the adoption of a new symbolic content for particular values, there were in Chile other important bases of solidarity for transforming the imposed statutes into legitimate norms. These included another value – the common welfare – affective ties, reciprocity, with its accompanying social control, and finally, charismatic leadership. A personal, affective relationship exists with such a leader; people will not desert him and if he says that a thing must be done then it is done. He makes the norms appear more legitimate by imbuing them with a religious or political aura. From Brazil in particular examples have emerged of charismatic leaders, religious prophets, who succeeded in changing the behaviour of large groups of peasants in a comparatively short time (Queiroz, 1965). Chile did possess peasant leaders with some charisma, but their message was political, not religious and they did not found any independent communities. Their charisma had influence, but in a smaller circle, among those with whom they had considerable contact as administrators. To these people they offered an example and probably some of their values rubbed off on them.

– Very little is known as yet about the way in which the circle of people with whom one identifies enlarges. Generally speaking this identification is preceded by economic integration. Sociological literature speaks of the lengthening of the chains of interdependence (Elias, 1969) and of the emergence of organic solidarity as the division of labour progresses. Anthropologists speak of an extension of the 'moral community'. In cultures where the chains of interdependence have grown long, the socialization of children appears to be accompanied by a tendency to accept responsibility which relates not so much to existing groups or associations but to membership of associations in the abstract. This trend then automatically embraces whatever new associations the individual may join; the act of becoming a member implies that the individual will comply with the obtaining concrete norms.

8.4 Factors which influence solidarity

In this section I intend, with the aid of examples derived from the practice of Chilean peasant organizations, to illustrate those factors which either help or hinder the growth of solidarity among members. It must be observed that in actual practice, several factors are involved at one and the same time. The accompanying diagram is intended primarily to give a comprehensive view of the main factors which appeared to contribute positively or negatively to solidarity. Since the organizations were still in an initial stage of development there was not yet much question of differentiation among the members. The problem was rather one of mechanical solidarity (giving more) than of organic (allowing the other to take more).

As qualitative research methods were employed to study this problem the arrows indicate positive or negative correlations which I imagine would be discovered if the variables were measured quantitatively. They are in fact hypotheses.

8.4.1 The instrumental value of the association

In an earlier section we distinguished between the act of co-operation performed out of self-interest and that which involves a sacrifice of resources. Although it is difficult to render this distinction operational, I am convinced that member solidarity was noticably greater wherever there was a clearer *identity between self-interest and communal in-*

106

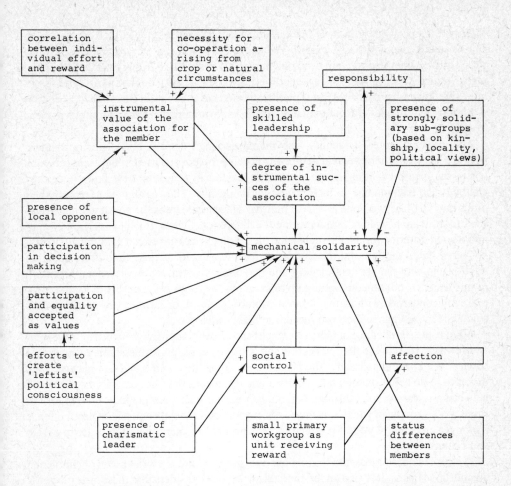

terest. I have already remarked on several occasions that the main reason why my agricultural worker informants accepted a communal farm was their expectation of material progress for themselves. The economic success of a peasant organization is chiefly important because on it depends the acceptance of the organization by the members and their solidarity. When I asked the small peasant farmers whether they would be prepared to co-operate in the communal exploitation of a fundo if invited, their affirmative answer was very often couched in terms of self-interest: 'That way at least I'd have something of my own', 'that would mean more land', 'we'd get more credit', 'it would be the only way to get some capital', or 'yes, for we'll turn them into individual farms'.

Identity of interests is also clear *where the possibility of individual progress is lacking.* INDAP personnel repeatedly noticed that the small, independent peasants appeared more inclined towards co-operation in the isolated areas of a province where natural circumstances were less favourable than in the areas close to the large cities. There also seemed to be a greater inclination towards co-operation on farms where (part of) the production process displayed the character of indivisibility, that is to say, *had* to be achieved through co-operation. In other words willingness to co-operate seemed greater

107

wherever the possibility of an *individual* solution to problems appeared less. The same can be said of the numerous, wide-spread examples which came to my notice of groups which had co-operated to build a school, improve a road, hire a truck. Many of my informants thought indeed that this co-operation could easily be focussed upon other goals but I thought rather that such examples concerned cases in which, for some local reason or another, communal and individual interests had overlapped in a manner that was clear to all.

The clarity of interest identity also increases when there is a stronger correlation between individual achievement and reward. This problem occurred in the asentamientos where the members were said to show little interest in acquiring new skills since they claimed such training did not better their lot financially. They continued to receive their day's pay just like everyone else. In a number of asentamientos the peasants themselves tried to draw up a scale of remuneration for different activities. It isn't easy, however, to find a good criterion for such a scale once the market prices have been abandoned. It cannot be disputed though that the asentados felt the need for a closer and more accurate relationship between personal reward and personal achievement. A very clear indication of this was the spontaneous setting up of small work groups in a number of asentamientos, each concerned with running one section of the farm, or farming one section of the land. The more their section produced, the higher their pay.

What is the significance of this preference for a close relationship between achievement and reward? It is, in the first place, that the achievement is performed with a view to the reward. We knew this already; the peasants accepted the communal farm because they expected to do better out of it materially. But it also means that the peasants distinguished between a reward earned through personal effort and a share in the joint production. In small work groups, in which it is much easier to exercise social control, the production is no longer a collective good for which there is no need to exert oneself in order to obtain one's share[4].

The care lavished by asentados on their own piece of land is a well known phenomenon on collective farms. It is also understandable when one considers that these little plots, the produce of which is not a collective good in Olson's sense, contribute a large share of the family income.

During the Frei period there were asentamientos where up to $\frac{2}{3}$ of the family income was produced on these pieces of land (de Ranitz & de Ranitz, 1972)[5]. In an economic study of 16 asentamientos, Jolly *et al.* (1970, p. 32) found that the income produced on individual pieces of land or using the peasant's own animals constituted on the average 23% of the gross family income. It is the wives in particular who urge their husbands not to neglect the family plot. Not only are they less familiar with the running of the asentamiento, they have no participating role in it either; they represent the family interest. Thus, this conflict of interests becomes at the same time a conflict of solidarity. This much becomes evident from the remarkable fact that in some asentamientos the machines belonging to the collective farm could be used gratis for tilling the privately worked pieces of land. This is a concealed subsidy on the part of the collectivity to the individual members and can only be explained by assuming that everyone is convinced of the legitimacy of working for the family interest.

There is yet another example. In a certain asentamiento the general council decided against making the sons of the asentados socios laborales (employee with certain rights), arguing that some families (with many adult sons) would have a considerable advantage over others (with only a few sons). This decision shows very clearly that the asentados recognized both a clash of interests and a conflict of solidarity.

The fact that the conflict of interests proceeds in part from the character of collective good possessed by the product of the asentamiento, appears from a complaint frequently made by asentados. They felt victimized by the lazy workers, those who skimped their work but still received the same payment from the administration. Clearly this argument could easily turn into a rationalization for the good workers to do less than their best. The diverse observations devoted by Lehmann (1972) to some of the above-mentioned phenomena, show that the tension persisted under Allende's regime.

In other associations – co-operatives and syndicates – the clash of interests between the individual (family) and the collectivity, assumed more the character of a conflict of solidarity. I encountered quite a number of peasant leaders who said that their wives were not very favourably impressed by their activities since these sometimes entailed a couple of weeks absence from home, or the neglect of their own private little pieces of land. One of them said that his friends and neighbours helped him on his farm, another that his wife objected to his seeking re-election in one particular year. A third – a member of a syndicate board – calculated for me how much he had lost financially during a year on the board, while others merely complained about this but didn't mention any figures. A leader – at national level – said that if he were married, he would never be able to devote so much time to his administrative work unless he received adequate recompense. The landowners too exploited this conflict of interests, notably by provoking it deliberately. In several cases the wives of the agricultural workers were persuaded to use their influence to prevent their husbands from organizing. It also occurred – although these were exceptional cases – that a leader was bribed by the owner: a larger piece of land was placed at his disposal or he was offered better terms of employment. On some of the farms – often the smaller ones – the owner made sure that his wage rise was just a little higher than that demanded by the syndicate. There were farms which made it their policy to treat their workers so well that the arguments of the syndical organizers fell upon deaf ears. The syndicate members themselves had the general feeling that the non-members on the farms were favoured, given the easiest jobs and better working conditions.

8.4.2   The common opponent

The existence of an obvious common opponent can also underline the identity of interests and lead to increased solidarity. Many of my informants observed that the syndicate ran in cycles of activity and lull. The activity was concentrated in those months in which new wage demands were drawn up and discussed with the members – and a new collective working arrangement was agreed upon with the landowners in the community. Such activities not infrequently terminated in a strike. During other conflicts too, such as the occupation of farms, the members displayed a large measure of solidarity, but once peace was signed the syndicate might spend months just barely ticking over. During conflicts, group action, with the visible emotionality and social control involved and the participating role of the women, in short, the dramatized identity of interests, was undoubtedly a factor conducive to solidarity.

8.4.3   Support for certain values: equality, justice, participation

The most solidary peasants I encountered in Chile were individuals who wanted to realize these three values for all peasants. In nearly every case they were also leaders, that is to say, their solidarity was rewarded with a high position. They were rather exceptional. Generally speaking, the new, peasantry-wide goals derived from these values were not deemed important by the majority of peasants. This does not mean that they advocated inequality or non-participation, but they acted as though the new ways of striving for equality, justice and participation were matters of no particular concern to them. A good deal of work would have to be done to jolt them into awareness. Taken in general the way in which these values were propagated by the promotors of INDAP and other organizations left much to be desired. They seemed to rely on something in the nature of a sermon which might be of a religious or political nature according to the conviction of the promotor, but which, so far as the peasants were concerned, seemed to go in one ear and out the other. Much more effective was the example which some leaders – and a few of the promotors – gave. It consisted of action, not talk, although they made their opinions clear as well. Their example inspired imitation among other individuals, rather than among the group as a whole. Psychologists have indeed discovered that altruistic behaviour can be promoted by example (cf. Wright, 1971, pp. 134–135).

It did not always appear necessary that an entire group should cherish these values. There were cases in which a committee, two or three people, persuaded their association to show solidarity with another group. There were others in which the committee of a municipal syndicate managed to organize a successful strike in protest against the dismissal of one single man somewhere on a fundo, a man completely unknown to 90% of the members. In these cases a suggestion made by Etzioni (1968, p. 101) in a somewhat different connection seems valid. He suggests that cohesion between the members of different associations is a function of the cohesion between their leaders. This was certainly true in those cases which I observed myself.

8.4.4   Affection

For the majority of Chilean peasants, affection seemed an important factor in promoting solidarity. It was not so much that the affection between the members of associations or collectivities was in any way remarkable, but rather that the contrary of affection – mistrust, antipathy – could seriously weaken an organization. In Chapter 6 we saw already that a person's affiliation to a co-operative or syndicate was often accompanied by the affiliation of his friends and relatives. It is the group of friends or relatives that joins. For an explanation of this we must turn to Simmel (1969) who observed that membership in two groups like this is not individualizing. A conflict of solidarity may still occur if the larger group wishes to go one way and the smaller another, but it is not acute from the very outset. This idea is interpreted in a very pregnant fashion by a respondent who had left the syndicate again: 'I felt lonely, I was the only one from home who had joined.' It may well be that, as Etzioni (1968, p. 100 ff) asserts, the affective relationships within sub-groups foster the cohesion of the association, that one is dealing with an expansion of the affective relationships.

The importance of affection within small groups: board members of associations, small committees, small production groups, was clear. The observer becomes aware that the committees and groups which function well are those in which most of the members are bound by ties of affection. Many of the small production groups which came into being through co-option, consisted of relatives, friends, and the odd neighbour. The reason given for this is 'these are people I can trust'. In the best committees I observed at work the affection between the members was obvious.

The difficulties arise when affection dies, either because people begin to mistrust each other regardless or to suspect each other of laziness, justifiably or not. This happens when functional demands are made upon the co-operative effort for which the affective group possesses no norms. The group then loses the ability to work well together. In one production group where there was not enough work to give everyone a full day's employment tensions ran so high that shots were fired (they fortunately missed). In another, which had started out very enthusiastically, a breach threatened between the younger and the older members. A number of the younger members wanted to leave. In yet another there was a whole drama when a pig was found to be missing after the return of one of the members who had been absent. The committees too, especially those of the co-operatives, can prove breeding grounds for suspicion. One or more of the members may have to visit Santiago or the provincial capital once a week for business with various government offices. For this he is given expense money and the others suspect him of lining his own pockets with it. He is suspect too because these visits teach him the bureaucratic tricks of the trade and make him indispensable. (In one case I came across this was in fact done deliberately. The chairman made the man who had accompanied him wait in the corridor until he had finished his conversation with the official.) Finally there is the question of politics, which we will return to later.

Affection is much more a relationship between individuals than between role bearers. We have already pointed out that Chilean peasants were hardly able to offer criticism – or accept it – as bearers of a role. The person criticized considered that he had suffered an injury to the honour and dignity of his entire person, instead of merely one aspect of it. He reacted to criticism with rage, disappointment, threats that he would chuck the job or with a counter attack. Affection makes criticism of role fulfillment even more difficult than it already is. Whereas in the preceding paragraphs we recognized the advantages of working in small co-operative units, the prominent role which affection plays here as the basis of solidarity is more of a disadvantage.

It was also true that the effectiveness of the promotors of INDAP and CORA depended upon their personal relationships with the peasants. They too could make themselves disliked and mistrusted, but they had one advantage. It was from them that all kinds of governmental favours flowed and so the peasants, up to a certain point, had to keep on the right side of them.

Yet affection need not permanently determine solidarity in this way. We asked the agricultural workers whom we had been researching to arrange in sequence a number of groups and collectivities according to the ties they felt with them. The interesting fact is that those members who claimed most solidarity with the campesinos (the peasant class), tended more often, in comparison with the rest, to have friends who were not themselves members of the syndicate (25% against 4.4% and 4.6%) and less often to have relatives on the fundo who were all members themselves (16% against 24% and 45%). This may indicate that peasant class awareness may replace affection as a motive for affiliation.

Such class conscious people join without bothering what their friends and relatives do: that is up to them. Even if they don't join this is evidently no reason for ending the friendship.

8.4.5 *Compensations: reciprocity, prestige, leadership and suspicion*

Solidarity is a gift which creates an obligation. This obligation may be redeemed in two ways; by evincing reciprocity or by conferring prestige upon the giver.

The importance of reciprocity became particularly clear at the moment it was found to be lacking. A committee member might feel deeply disappointed if the members did not fulfil their obligations, if for instance they ignored the committee's summons to come and help rebuilding a shed, or failed to attend meetings. Not only did he think that they had fallen down on their obligation; he also appeared to feel himself absolved of his own obligation. The feeling of being put upon, which could spring up very easily in production groups, could in fact frequently be traced back to a lack of reciprocity, real or imagined, to the idea that the other person was doing less than he ought. Prestige is a reward conferred upon those who render considerable service to a group. On a hacienda it is the person who openly urges resistance to the patron, who shows himself unafraid of reprisals and who is capable of standing up for himself during negotiations. In the asentamientos it is he who displays the best managerial qualities. In the co-operatives these qualities are important too, but co-operatives remain much more dependent on governmental support. Very few board members of co-operatives had the vision, the organizing talent and the perseverance to start up and nurse along an organization embracing one or more communities and capable of becoming a very large enterprise indeed. Many board members were indeed convinced of the necessity for co-operation, were very zealous and dedicated in preaching the good news and in founding an organization, but were then at a loss what to do next. They took the prestige they received as their due, they allowed themselves to be elected and sent as delegates to assemblies of federative associations, they spoke of their sacrifices, but for the rest they were less than effective. And yet, more than once, it appeared that this kind of man had already attempted in the past to set up a co-operative in his community. He meant well, but had no idea how to proceed once the co-operative was actually there, and it sometimes seemed that by heaping him with prestige, the members had also rendered him harmless; they had fulfilled their obligations.

In a couple of cases, however, such a board member – often the chairman – did have ideas on how to proceed. A tractor was then bought in common, or a truck; an abattoir was built or a good project drawn up in order to obtain credit from INDAP. In these cases the leaders often had something charismatic about them: they exuded forcefulness. Since they did more, the members had to do more in return; the mere granting of prestige was not enough. Another leader said of himself that he acted like a dictator in his committee. He himself set about collecting contributions, and refused to be fobbed off. However, he also made sure that the necessary production inputs were available. He asked INDAP for twice as much as the members of his committee had requested him. If there was a shortage then of, for instance, salitre later in the year, he could say to a non-member: why don't you join and I'll see that you get 40 sacks of salitre tomorrow (not in a month, or in a week, but tomorrow!). He made good his promise too, so that the person in question was left standing open-mouthed. He had in consequence a considerable hold over his people. The members of the committee paid back their loans, attended meetings and paid up their fees. This kind of leader often succeeded in turning the co-operative into a not inconsiderable 'business'. The objection, however, was that he made himself indispensable. Sometimes he was not aware of this. He was so preoccupied with the budding business and so afraid of seeing what he had built up destroyed, that he couldn't bring himself to run the risk that others might make the wrong decisions. Sometimes, though, it was deliberate policy. The leader then monopolized information, took the credit for what another committee member had done, played off different local groups against each other and allowed himself to be re-elected in spite of opposition.

I attended a meeting of a board which had one of these almost charismatic leaders as its chairman, and it was plain to see that the leader had his fellow board members on a tight rein. There was no agenda; he decided what was to be discussed. Every point in the agenda inspired him to one or more long and often amusing anecdotes. Throughout all this his fellow board members clearly showed their impatience; one of them even began to read the newspaper. And yet it was always the leader who announced that they were about to proceed to the next point. Such 'indispensable' leaders hamper member participation and thus the necessary training of fellow board members. 'They are really essential at the beginning,' said an INDAP promotor, 'but later it is impossible to get them to work democratically and to take pride in making themselves dispensable'[6].

Dependence upon one man is dangerous for an organization, if only because that man is not invulnerable. He can make a mistaken decision, with which he must be identified by virtue of his position. A mistake like this relieves the others of some of their obligation and they feel justified in becoming less active. Another possibility is that the co-operative becomes so large that local shopkeepers and tradesmen feel their interests threatened and grow hostile. Their hostility will certainly take the form of spreading rumours and gossip about the leader. Once such a campaign has begun the members are under pressure from different sides to believe one version of a story or another.

Suspicion is constantly lurking. In actual fact our quantitative data on leaders showed that, generally speaking, they had enjoyed certain advantages more than had the members. At one meeting – as a reaction on the part of the board of a co-operative to a piece of gossip doing the rounds – details were read out concerning those individuals for whom the lorry had driven during the past month, and what had been paid for the loads carried. It proved that by far the most of the trips had been for the chairman and manager of the co-operative. In this case the book-keeping was very competent but elsewhere it was quite common for appointments to be made by word of mouth, or notes to be scribbled on loose sheets of paper. This made it practically impossible for any ordinary member to distinguish any more between honesty and deception. Ready suspicion absolved the member from any further obligations towards the suspect leader. His solidarity was denied and so did not have to be reciprocated[7].

8.4.6 Social control

I have already pointed out that the peasants tended to criticize or receive criticism as individuals rather than as role-bearers. This made constructive criticism practically impossible. Often a grievance was bottled up for far too long and when it finally burst loose, a blazing quarrel immediately developed. The peasants have no idea how to return then to normal relationships, said an INDAP official.

The quarrels which may arise between two individuals are all the more disturbing since both parties appeal to the solidarity groups which support them, whether relatives or friends. In this way a conflict spreads very rapidly. The unintentional result of this was that in hardly a single co-operative did the official control commission function properly.

In a number of co-operatives there was no control either on the fulfilment of obligations such as the payment of the subscription in full. In one co-operative in Colchagua whose books I managed to look into, it appeared that only 2 or 3% of the members were fully paid up. Many members had paid only 10%, 20% or 50% of the money, and this was not because they had only recently joined. Most of them hadn't paid anything for two years. I estimated that the co-operative had still to get in about 70% of the amount owing, a sum large enough to pay for a couple of tractors.

If effective social control in the co-operative enterprises was often conspicuous by its absence, where it did occur it was sometimes quite drastic. In one co-operative which was flourishing quite well from the economic point of view, about ten members were expelled in the course of two years. Some of these were in fact founder-members. The two most frequent reasons given were that they had blackened the character of a board member or the manager, or that during harvest time they had not hired a threshing machine from the co-operative but had brought one in from outside. It was principally those leaders who acted out of strong ideological conviction who dared to exercise social control and thereby teetered on the edge of paternalism.

One of the best INDAP promotors I met in Chile told me that he had a certain method of intervening when things threatened to go wrong in the co-operative of which he was in charge. He waited until the situation was so desperate that at least the board and some of the members realized that the co-operative would fail if something weren't done quickly. This was when he stepped in with his suggestions. 'Only then are they willing to accept anything from you', he said. 'If you approach them earlier they won't listen.'

All this does not mean that there is hardly any social control. There is, but it is either non-verbal or takes the form of a passing joke or a story doing the rounds. Only seldom does the association apply its statutory sanctions. What social control there is is effective, but the indirect way in which it is applied means that it is particularly effective in smaller groups.

8.4.7 Braking factors: differences in status and sub-group solidarity

The mechanical solidarity of a group is impaired if differences in status occur among the members, that is, real or supposed differences in interest.

I encountered the following examples of categorical interest conflicts within the Chilean peasant associations. In the asentamientos there was the clear conflict between seasonal workers drawn from outside and the actual members. Cases occurred in which the asentados were as harsh in dealing with striking workers as had been the landed proprietors. They attempted to break the strike by mobilizing their wives and children to save the harvest. In most syndicates a conflict of interests developed if some of the members became asentados. The latter usually left the syndicate after a time, one of their reasons being that their contribution was no longer paid for them. Only occasionally did I encounter a group of asentados who considered it their duty to help their ex-colleagues become asentados themselves and for this reason remained in the syndicate. Frequently too those workers who preferred to remain on the patron's reserva rather than join the asentamiento, were to be found among the supervisory personnel. These had also been the highest paid workers on the fundo. De Ranitz & de Ranitz (1972) found that those asentados who had seen their relative advantage over their traditional groups of reference diminished were the least satisfied with land reform.

In the co-operatives there was some conflict of interest between agricultural workers and independent peasants on the one hand and between the co-operative as a whole and its component production groups on the other. The primary question was, to which tasks should the co-operative give priority, to providing cheap consumer goods or to bolstering up production. While not giving rise to actual conflict, this dilemma did cause some dissatisfaction. Unfortunately the position in Chile in 1970 was such that there was a certain danger in a co-operative attempting to provide that service most ardently desired by the poorest peasants and the agricultural workers, namely the sale of consumer goods. It might see its capital disappear as a result of inflation if it settled for a small profit margin. Although I have no figures at my disposal to support this assertion, I came across enough cases to hazard that a considerable percentage (20% or more) of the co-operatives had condemned themselves to non-activity in this way.

Such a categorical contrast assumed more dramatic forms in certain co-operatives in the province of Colchagua, the only co-operatives at the time to contain large production groups. Some of these groups held land while others had large chicken farms. According to the statutes, these groups were obliged to do all their business via the co-operative, which in some cases was also the nominal owner of the means of production. The co-operative, however, worked with one fund for all the services. This resulted in the credit balances of the production groups being used to provide a loan elsewhere, or pay off a debt, or to make some purchase or other. Then, when the groups wished to avail of their surplus, it could happen that there was not enough money in the kitty. Especially when poultry prices began to tumble and the groups to work at a loss, with the increasing danger that their supplies of feed would be cut off because of failure to pay, they started to buy and sell outside of the co-operatives.

A remarkable example of a growing difference in status and the estrangement which can result from it, is the following. A co-operative which had been set up a couple of years earlier in a small coastal village of the province of Santiago was extremely successful. With only limited credit it had built up a machine park, started a cattle fodder factory, was about to open a small sausage and meat factory. In addition it provided consumer goods for the members. The membership was continually expanding. However, although the co-operative was also open to young people, the working sons of the members, the latter were dissatisfied. They felt that the co-operative worked for their fathers, but did nothing for them. When then another government service which dealt particularly with young people started working in the village alongside INDAP, this dissatisfaction led to plans for setting up a second co-operative intended specially for the younger people. It only fell through because of resistance by INDAP.

The clash of interests between categories also played a part in the relationships between the various categorical organizations on the provincial or national level. I have frequently seen peasant leaders or politically interested outsiders attempt to achieve greater unity or to combine the forces of the various organizations. Their usual argument was that the peasants formed a class with a particular class interest. Not much seemed to result from all this during my stay in Chile. This was, it appeared, because there was no attempt to reach accurate and concrete agreement on co-operation, in other words, on promoting those interests which the categories really shared. Instead of recognizing that the categories also had opposing interests — for instance regarding the wage paid to agricultural workers — promotors hammered away at this all-embracing yet still vague notion of class interest[8].

Apart from differences in category we may also, on the basis of our theoretical analysis of Section 8.2 – expect a clash of interests to arise around the *distribution* of the product of co-operation. And such clashes did indeed occur in the co-operatives and the asentamientos, as well as in the federations which they joined. The most usual case concerned a local group which either did not wish to join a larger unit or else, having joined, was dissatisfied with the distribution. It was noteworthy, for instance, that sometimes only a quarter or less of the members of a local committee of small peasant-farmers joined the regional co-operative when the committee was officially incorporated into it. This might have been due in part to the financial sacrifice involved, though, as we already saw, very few paid the whole of the obligatory contributions. I think, therefore, that this hesitation must also be attributed to the recognition of a distribution problem.

Distribution problems arose in the co-operatives in connection with the priority given to certain tasks and the geographical location of development projects. Generally speaking if a co-operative wished to achieve a certain degree of viability, it had to earn money. This could only be done by first tackling those tasks which were to the advantage of the peasants who supplied most products for the market, i.e. the larger of the smallholders, from whose ranks indeed the board members were often drawn. This could lead to the emergence of two status groups of larger and smaller independent peasants. The latter might even turn away from the co-operative altogether, regarding it as the instrument of the other status groups (cf. Lehmann, 1970a and 1970b).

A distribution problem involving production groups arose in the province of Colchagua. There it frequently happened that a member of a production group was elected to the board of a higher organization such as a co-operative or the provincial federation of co-operatives. He then worked for that organization a couple of days a week. In the beginning he received no compensation for this, since the organizations had no money. This meant that the production group was supporting a member whose work contribution had declined, for the sake of the higher organization. In the end this so irritated the other members of the production group that they forbade their fellow members to remain on the board. The federation of Colchagua, a pioneer in many respects, resolved the difficulty by starting to pay such a board member for his work. The money was derived from the percentage it retained on transactions concluded through its intermediary and by skimming off a certain overhead from credits granted through the federation to the co-operatives. Both these methods of financing could lead in their turn to protests from the associated co-operatives. The federation required the board member in question to pay his earnings into the funds of his own production group which then paid him out the same as the other members received.

It was characteristic of the distribution problem in federative associations that the participating units were usually keen on having a representative on the board of the federation. He was then expected to do his best to influence distribution in favour of his unit of origin.

Generally speaking, when sub-groups harm the mechanical solidarity of the main group their material interests will also deviate from the common interest. One may count as exceptions those sub-groups whose bond of solidarity could indeed only be interpreted in cultural terms.

An innocent example is that of the peasant who goes out drinking with his friends in the evening and then the following day is incapable of putting in a good day's work on the communal farm. I have no quantitative data to show how frequently this occurred but I do know that in the province of Santiago, the managers of various asentamientos mentioned alcohol as the most important dysfunctional phenomenon. It was also significant that the sale of hard liquor within asentamientos was forbidden. This prohibition was evidently inspired by the fear that to sell drink so close to home would only encourage drunkenness.

Factions sometimes formed in asentamientos when two fundos were joined to make one asentamiento. These factions, so detrimental to solidarity, were usually political. In both co-operatives and asentamientos an atmosphere of mistrust and one-upmanship developed when such groups tried to obtain for themselves the majority on a board or the specialized committees of an association. The role of politics was so complex however, that it seems better to devote a separate section to it.

8.4.8   The role of politics

In order to illustrate the conflict of loyalties and the increase in solidarity to which politics can give rise it is necessary to delve a little deeper into the political situation in Chile in 1970. In Chapter 3 we have already seen that in Chile too, when the time seemed ripe to mobilize the peasants as political allies and electors, various political and ideological groupings set about the task. During the Frei government there were three large confederations of syndicates. One of these, Ranquil, was dominated by the socialists and communists. Another, El Triunfo Campesino, which consisted mainly of syndicates founded by INDAP, was linked to the Christian Democrats, as was the third, Libertad, which grew out of the syndicates set up by Catholic groups.

It may be argued that the very existence of three confederations in place of one already constituted a weakening of the peasants' position. This argument is reinforced every time they were unable to agree on a common course of action and either did nothing at all or else carried out the action with a section of the agricultural workers as mere spectators. On the other hand it is also true, as Etzioni (1968, p. 408) asserts, that when several associations fulfil the same function they keep each other on their toes and prevent, to some extent, countermobilization. However, as the confederations increasingly took it upon themselves to defend the policy of a particular party, their existence tended more to weaken the unity of the peasants. In view of the great differences in economic, social and family status among the peasants it is in my view unrealistic to suppose that all peasants will feel drawn to the same party, where four or five political parties compete for voters, members and supporters. The Chilean political parties (like almost all political parties in Latin America) were interest-agglomerations which originated in the towns. There was no real peasant party. Under these circumstances it is hardly surprising that the peasants divided up among three or four parties, chosing whichever they thought would suit their interests best. The communist party, the socialist party, the PDC, the Radicals and

MAPU each had their own supporters among the peasants, although in some cases these were few in number.

Division arose not so much because of differences of opinion among the peasants, as through the machinations of the parties. Each party tried to erect a political bastion by gaining control of leaders and by diverting government funds to the peasants, either for a project or as credit. More than a year before the presidential elections of 1970 the parties, and INDAP, as a government agency, appeared very much aware of what seemed to them the necessity of installing political supporters in those leadership posts open to election. This was achieved not so much by distorting results as by pressing through the candidature of certain persons. The question of who might prove the most capable leader was only secondary; the main thing was to get a party man elected. Given the fact that most of my participating research was carried out in organizations dominated, nominally at least, by the PDC (El Triunfo and the confederation of co-operatives) it was the PDC which I most frequently saw winning. This was achieved by sabotaging any capable peasant leader suspected of holding a different political conviction. The greatest sufferers among the leaders were the MAPU supporters. Thus, for instance, at the election of the board of El Triunfo at the end of 1969, a young charismatic leader from the north of the country – who was already a member of the board – was passed over for the chairmanship because he was said to belong to MAPU.

In December 1969, during the elections to the board of the Confederation of Peasant Co-operatives, the representative of the Federation of the province of Colchagua missed a seat by one vote. This scarcely appeared accidental. It happened despite the fact that his Federation was the furthest developed, had the most active and conscientous board, and was most acutely aware of the path which the organized small peasants should take. He was, however, regarded as a MAPU supporter. I have no doubt that all the parties played this little game, with the excuse that 'the others did it too'. During the last months before the elections such machinations rendered the normal working of the peasant organizations difficult if not impossible. INDAP too ceased to function. Employees who were considered politically unreliable were transferred from the field to the capital, or, if they were already stationed there, were refused a car to go out into the country. The available cars were used to transport political propagandists. The most incredible accusations of sabotage were circulated to explain why projects had failed.

This state of affairs gave rise to various kinds of solidarity conflict. A peasant leader starting to play a political role was obliged to choose at certain moments, when the interests of the peasants clashed with those of the party. The peasants themselves were uncertain whether they ought to show solidarity with other peasants because they were peasants too, or to refuse solidarity because they felt attracted to a different party.

Since none of the parties in Chile was a real peasant party, identification with one party also meant identification with interests which were not entirely those of the peasant. In this respect it is clear that the peasants were used to some extent by all the parties and would probably remain dependent whatever the result of the elections[9]. Even more paralyzing than what the peasants did, however, was their mistrust of what other peasants were suspected of doing. Every initiative on the part of somebody else was, in 1970 at least, interpreted as a political move intended to support one's own party to the detriment of others. I very often heard some leader accused of political activity, of blindly carrying out orders from some party headquarters, yet when I saw this person in action I was unable, with the best will in the world, to detect any proselytism. It may be that this suspicion was particularly rife in 1970, an important election year.

The indications that the peasants' votes can be bought by a particularistic expenditure of government funds are ambiguous. We ourselves found, in an ecological analysis of the results of the presidential election of 1970, that the extent to which land reform had been carried out in a community had not benefited Tomic, the candidate of the party in power. It did, however, seem as though the category of peasants who had most improved their position during Frei's government, the inquilinos and the permanent workers, had opted for Tomic (cf. Galjart, 1974). An analysis of the losses suffered by the PDC between the congress elections of 1965 and the municipal elections of 1967 indicates that the different categories of peasants had reacted differently to the land reform, according to whether they had benefited by it or not (Kaufman, 1972, p. 124 ff).

An anonymous analysis of the congress by-elections of 1972 in the provinces of Maule, Colchagua and O'Higgins showed no link at all between the percentage of votes gained by the Unidad Popular and the favours which this party had dispensed locally. The most probable explanation is that the various categories of smallholders and agricultural workers felt that they had benefited to varying degrees and this was reflected in their votes. Whatever the explanation, in 1970 not only the parties, but the peasants as well, were convinced that patronage produced votes. And although almost everyone agreed that politics divided them, they had no option but to follow their respective parties. Lacking any authentic view of their own on the future of rural Chile they were obliged to look to the parties for it.

8.5 Solutions

There are various ways in which a person torn by conflicting norms can resolve his problem, assuming that he himself, and others, recognize what is wrong. Failure to do so through a compartmentalization of roles for instance, is also a kind of solution; it prevents eruptions but may also halt the process of dawning awareness. Thompson & Van Houten (1970, p. 147 ff) suggest the following possibilities: expanding or cutting down on the *number of positions* one has, *transferring responsibilities* to another and *negotiating a compromise*. What significance might these proposals have in the context of co-operation in Chile? We begin by noting that, if conflicts of solidarity are linked with roles, as we postulated, the roles, and thus the conflicts, cannot be expected to disappear of their own accord.

The first possibility would imply the removal of functions from the family and other primary groups, thus rendering the role of father, of friend, of party member etc., less demanding. I consider this to be possible only in a limited number of cases, for example where two local groups share an asentamiento. Then certain measures can be taken to weaken the importance of this bonding principle. But for the time being I cannot imagine the family losing any of its functions. In practice this possibility also implies attributing more weight to one position than to the other and thus living up to one norm but not to the other. In other words, one might favour one group, of which one is a member, over another. In this respect do people distinguish between groups? When requested to list the various groups and categories according to the strength of their attachment to them the respondents gave consistent replies. Table 26 shows the average positions attributed to

Table 26. Average attachment of members and non-members of syndicates to various groups of which they are members (average positions)

Category of respondents	Attachment to						N
	family	blood relatives	the Chilean people	workers on the fundo	the peasants	the working class	
All members	1.47	3.38	3.17	3.67	3.94	5.37	143
All non-members	1.56	3.08	2.76	3.80	4.46	5.34	67
Ex-members	1.22	2.97	2.99	3.65	4.60	5.57	35
Never-members	1.93	3.21	2.50	3.96	4.31	5.09	32
Leaders	1.56	3.46	3.78	3.43	4.02	4.75	41
Other members	1.44	3.35	2.93	3.76	3.91	5.61	102

the groups by agricultural workers.

The table shows that it is precisely the classes (the peasants and the working class) which come last. The sequence of the groups correlates with the degree to which these relationships possess a face-to-face character, with one exception, the Chilean people. The weight attributed to face-to-face relationships indicates that solidarity is indeed to a large extent determined by affection and interaction. It also underlines our earlier argument that individuals who become involved in a conflict can mobilize their primary groups and thus cause dissention between groups. The table indicates too how conflicts of solidarity will probably be decided, should they arise.

Although the members and non-members of co-operatives also put their family first, the other groups were ranked differently by different respondents. As a result the average positions of these groups are about the same.

In many countries a conflict of solidarity was avoided, in co-operatives at least, by handing over responsibility to paid employees. The members' sacrifice was then limited to a financial contribution. This, however, led to those individuals in managerial positions forming an oligarchy. In Chile such a solution would have been too expensive and would also have detracted from the members' participation in decision making.

Another form of transfer of responsibility was frequently applied in Chile without the peasants being really aware of it. I refer to the habit of blaming the government for anything that goes wrong. It is very difficult to draw the line between situations in which the opinion that one is dependent on the government and thus ultimately absolved of responsibility is correct and situations in which it is not. The examples of what really strong, animated leaders managed to accomplish prove that some felt this dependence less than others. Besides, although such an idea might be justified it clearly resulted in both leaders and members regarding themselves as absolved from all blame in advance. This is illustrated by the decline of a co-operative described in Chapter 5. It is clear that so long as the government continues to pre-occupy itself so directly with the doings of co-operative enterprises, this avenue of escape from solidarity conflicts will remain open.

The most important of the possible solutions to such conflicts remains then a negotiated change in role, a compromise. These negotiations did occur. In the asentamientos for example, an ever-recurring point on the agenda was the question of how large the piece of land for private use (the goce) ought to be, and how many privately owned head of cattle one might be allowed to graze (the talaje). After 1970, the government of the Unidad Popular attempted to cut back on the goce and talaje, but without much success (Lehmann, 1972). We have also seen already how managers, criticized by the members for having abused their position, often reacted by threatening to resign. This too is a form of negotiation about role content, although the parties may not see it in this light.

8.6 Recommendations

It might be useful to list the recommendations we have made in the course of this chapter and to add a few others. Our theory concerning interest clashes and solidarity conflicts implies that we regard them as permanent. Even if, under certain circumstances, the majority, or a considerable minority of the peasants – for instance the temporary workers who up to 1970 fared worst in the land reform – should act for a time as a class in order to achieve a particular aim, this would not mean an end to later clashes and conflicts of solidarity.

Our first recommendation would accordingly be, that the urban intellectuals who have guided the process of land reform, should recognize that such conflicts are a permanent feature. Only then will it be possible to search for those types of organization which would limit the damage to a minimum. Some intellectuals are convinced that, if only pressure could be exerted to press through a particular institutional structure, the difficulties would be bound to disappear. But this is only partly correct. An asentado who no longer has a little plot of land for his own use can no longer work it. Yet it would be naive to assume that this would eliminate the conflict of interests between family and collectivity. There are still a number of ways in which the asentado can favour his family at the expense of the collectivity. In other words, although a number of contrasts and solidarity conflicts might disappear, most of them would change in form only.

With respect to the communal farms, production groups or associations, my recommendations amount to the following.
– Since solidarity may depend upon the economic interests of the participants in an association, it is of the utmost importance that the association should serve these interests well. While high agricultural production may be important for society as a whole, its chief significance lies in binding together the members of the communal farm, the production group or the association. This places demands both on the capabilities of farm managers and leaders and on the functioning of the government services.
– Incentives should be provided for maximum achievement. This means that achievement and reward would be more closely linked and also that skilled work would be better rewarded than unskilled. Generally speaking it would also require small work-units so that the members could keep check on each other. The optimum group composition could be obtained through a system of co-option. For functions less suited to a small group – I am thinking of units of from six to ten families – such units could be joined together, each having a representative on the board in charge of that particular function.
– Instead of preaching unity, it should be explained to these – and other – associations, that members have many interests in common but also some that conflict, so that conflicts of solidarity may arise. The members should be taught to discuss their difficulties openly

121

beforehand and also when such a conflict has grown acute, so that a solution acceptable to all may be arrived at. This lengthy process of mutual accommodation may also be used to draw up rules for cases not provided for by domestic regulations and to transform these rules into legitimate norms.

– All this implies that the peasants must learn to accept and to offer criticism. Those who will have to teach this to the peasants will require an attitude which, however permeated with political ideology, is nonetheless sympathetic. One way of introducing these ideas to the peasants, without much effort on their part, is the socio-drama.

– The technique of holding meetings must be improved. Established procedures will have to be followed with regard to the agenda and the provision of information. Those who are to have charge of the meetings must be trained.

All these recommendations amount to a redefinition of roles to allow for compromise. On the other hand we also stress the creation of conditions (awareness, patience) which favour such compromises and which make them seem worthwhile to the peasants.

My recommendations with respect to the relations between associations and within the peasant class are the following.

– We are concerned here with the internalization of norms derived from values such as justice, equality and solidarity. I have already remarked in a previous section that I do not believe in the result of preaching, nor in the glossing over of division in order to emphasize unity. Leaders who recognize these values and act upon them achieve a powerful effect. The question is, can such leaders be cultivated? The attempt could at least be made; in any case it is worthwhile to be always on the lookout for their appearance.

– It seems advisable to set up local councils in which the various categories of peasants are all represented. These would be in a position to draw up plans and take decisions regarding land reform, credit, the sale and manufacture of products, investment priority, working facilities etc. The result would be that the representatives of the various categories and their organizations would be compelled to take each other and each other's interests into account. Should they fail to do so a stalemate develops which is to no one's advantage. Obliged constantly to consult with and account to those they represented, the latter too would learn the necessity for taking the interests of other categories of peasants to heart. The council could begin by listing and studying the problems of agriculture within the community. These problems – and their possible solutions – could then be discussed with the peasants, at meetings. The government of the Unidad Popular has indeed set up committees such as these. According to one analysis they work well, provided they do not break up along party lines. Another author, however, hints that the government does not really allow them to take many decisions (Lehmann, 1972). This is understandable, since the peasants often lack the necessary technical knowledge. Yet if the government continues to decide for them, the different categories of peasants encounter each other only as rivals, each concerned only with acquiring the lion's share of whatever funds are available. It seems to me that if a government wishes these peasant co-operative endeavours to succeed without exercising too much coercion, the most advisable course would be to leave quite a large number of decisions to the committees.

Notes

1 In the case of the Chilean asentamientos there were additional circumstances which gave the product the character of a collective good. There was, for instance, the fact that CORA advanced credit in order to meet the daily wages. On paper this was an advance on profit still to be realized, but in practice it took a year or longer to tot up the balance of profit or loss. The advance thereby acquired the character of a loan which ultimately had little connection with the results achieved by the farm. Besides, since the market value of various kinds of work had been abandoned only the hours actually worked were paid for, and no account was taken of the quality of the work or the effort put into it.

2 For that matter, Friedrichs himself found indications that 'the expression of altruism towards ingroup members is not likely to be accompanied by its expression toward outgroup members' (*op. cit.*, p. 504).

3 It is interesting that in the Kibbutz, a group which lays a very high permanent claim upon the solidarity of the members, functions are withdrawn from other groups, notably the family. Part of the care for the education of the children is entrusted to the Kibbutz itself (see also Barkin & Bennett, 1972).

4 The problem of the necessity for a material incentive is a constantly recurring point of discussion in socialist countries. One of the most recent of such discussions took place in Cuba, between none other than Ernesto Guevara, Charles Bettelheim, and Ernest Mandel. (For a German translation see De Santis, 1969). For my part I believe that a material incentive is essential, especially since the clash of interests between individual and collectivity is closely linked with a conflict of solidarity between family and collectivity. However, the family as an institution shows no signs of dying out in any socialist country. It is not by chance that the Israeli Kibbutz deprived the family of some of its functions. In so doing it also detracted from the insistent character of family solidarity.

5 Mr. and Mrs. de Ranitz spent a period of five months on three asentamientos in the province of Aconcagua.

6 It may be useful to refer here to the interesting hypothesis of Morais (1969) who says that, in contrast to agricultural labourers, independent peasants do not function well in an organization based upon a division of labour, since they are used to tackling everything themselves. They shove everything off onto a leader who in this way becomes a sort of despot. In other words, he does everything himself and refuses to delegate, and even if he does delegate he neglects to check up on the work. He is held accountable for failures and any failures cost him prestige.

   My own data do not contradict this hypothesis. It was a fact that the syndicate leaders were better able to divide up the work among themselves than were the co-operative managers. My explanation, however, is more prosaic than that of Morais. The syndicates were governed by legal regulations and provisions which rendered a division of labour both possible and necessary. The co-operatives were not. Often they couldn't pay even one board member.

7 I therefore do not agree with Lehmann (1969) when he says that the peasants are particularly suspicious of outsiders. It seems to me that they are also extremely suspicious of each other.

8 After having made myself unpopular on one occasion by drawing attention to the clash of interests which indeed existed, for the rest of the time I kept my peace. Nonetheless, I found it a pity – and still do – that anyone who urges that such a conflict be taken into acount is looked upon as a trouble-maker or even a political opponent, while he may perhaps be able to bring more real insight to bear on the situation than a person who believes blindly in class-consciousness. It is not by chance that Alberti (1972) makes the distinction between peasant behaviour which only appears to be inspired by class and behaviour which actually is.

9 This prediction proved incorrect in the first instance. During the period of Allende's government the peasant organizations, and in particular the asentamientos, began to show increasing independence of the government. For the government itself, this had dysfunctional results which in the course of time would probably have provoked a reaction.

Epilogue: Theoretical and practical conclusions for policy-makers

In this epilogue I should like to mention, very briefly, the various theoretical and practical conclusions I arrived at on the basis of my research. I must warn the reader that I am by no means certain that my conclusions are always correct. Still, even a sociologist should be willing to stick his neck out if the occasion demands. The conclusions outlined here are those which I would venture to advance should I be asked to advise some policy-making body.

1. With regard to peasant mobilization it would appear that, while certain factors may help or hinder it, the attitude of the government is critical for the outcome. An antagonistic, oppressive government can prevent the peasants from ever achieving a strong organization. This places a special responsibility upon the government. In countries where the peasants are not organized, this can, in my opinion, be imputed to government oppression. The power of the large landowners alone would not be sufficient explanation for this.

2. Although, in the initial phase of organization, the peasants may sometimes appear to constitute a revolutionary force, they are in fact solely concerned with depriving a particular category of people of their power to dispose of land which in their opinion should be divided up amongst themselves. Once land reform has been carried out the peasants prove the most fervent supporters of a situation in which the private possession of the means of production predominates. It is precisely in those countries in which the government desires to retain this private basis of production organization (Brazil, for example) that a rapid, radical programme of land reform would gain it millions upon millions of supporters (cf. Petras & Zemelman, 1972).

3. The existence of inequality is not in itself sufficient to cause the disadvantaged to revolt. The changes outlined in Chapter 3 are *essential* if the poor, disadvantaged or backward peasants are to be aroused. In the words of Young (1970) and Lamond Tullis (1970) it is necessary that the potential possibilities should outstrip the capacity of availing of them if the peasants (or any other group in the same circumstances) are to band together to remove this structural impediment. This also implies, however, that those who desire structural change must view with a benevolent eye any development which leads to inequality.

4. In a region devoid of extensive properties where there is no question of land reform nor of the redistribution of land, the mobilization of the small peasant producers is frequently reflected in service co-operatives set up by the government. Such co-operatives have very

little chance of success; they lack capital and competent leadership and the members are often as yet incapable of appreciating the necessity for collaboration. It would, in any case, be illusory to imagine that a simple service co-operative would be sufficient to counter existing social inequality and the poverty of the poorest.

With a production co-operative of any size, the situation is different. Although, to begin with, the peasants will always tend to resist the joining together of land, it may gain acceptance provided that the economic results attained by the co-operative surpass what might be expected from individual exploitation. Apart from natural circumstances this depends chiefly upon the quality of the management. Management training is thus of the utmost importance.

5. It is recommended that service co-operatives should be set up especially in places where groups of peasants experience a situation of 'structural bind'. In other words the social structure prevents them from utilizing the available development possibilities. Such groups need not be based on class. They may be brought together by age or because they differ in religion or ethnic origin from the surrounding peasant population. The required mechanical solidarity is then based upon a desire to improve one's lot which the individual finds impossible to fulfil on his own, while obstacles to this fulfilment are plainly evident in the social structure.

6. Where there can be no question of utilizing a 'structural bind' (this also occurs where there is no obvious local opponent), it is recommended that a start should be made in co-operation on the basis of small groups brought into being by co-option. When one group is insufficient to ensure a certain service function, the groups may merge into larger associations in which all the component groups have their say through a representative.

7. With regard to production co-operatives it is also preferable that the basic units, i.e. the units whose achievements are rewarded proportionately, should remain small. I am thinking of units comprising six to ten members (cf. Klatzmann, 1972). This promotes mechanical solidarity by means of affection, social control and the instrumental value of the association.

8. Both service and production co-operatives can best develop further by undertaking the processing of products and the manufacture of inputs themselves. The government must promote this development.

9. Member solidarity with or, as the case may be, in their association depends to a large extent on their real involvement in decision-making. At the end of the previous chapter we made certain recommendations concerning improved exchange of ideas and the offering of criticism. These chiefly involve the participants living up to their roles.

10. A number of the foregoing conclusions imply that, in a situation of social inequality (situation B, in the terms of Chapter 3) it is extremely difficult, if not impossible, to improve the lot of the poorest smallholders without making a problem of inequality itself and thus laying stress on the class position of these peasants. In other words, in the absence of a 'structural bind' of, for instance, a religious nature, the development of the

125

poorest peasants involves a political choice directed against certain elements or mechanisms within that society. Unless this fact is recognized, development work in the interests of the poorer peasants may well come to a standstill when the necessity for such a political choice becomes evident.

It is essential then that the peasants should be made aware of their position as a class. They should be taught to appreciate their relationship with other categories and the way in which they are incorporated into the political and economic system as a whole. Only those who possess this awareness are capable of trying to change their situation. Unfortunately, though, success cannot be guaranteed.

11. Success or failure in service and production co-operatives is determined by their economic achievements. These, in their turn, are largely dependent upon the quality of the leadership and management. It would seem inadvisable for a government to take over the task of management entirely, since this would have an adverse effect upon participation. In any case it is doubtful whether the government itself would possess personnel of sufficient calibre. In addition to training the peasants to take over as managers, I think it would be worthwhile considering the creation of a small number of very highly skilled teams of consultants. These teams could then use their technical and organizing talents to assist the peasant communities in putting into operation schemes drawn up by themselves. This would prevent a situation in which the government's available technical expertise – and this includes the economists and sociologists – would have to be spread too thinly over too large an area.

References

Affonso, A., S. Gomez, E. Klein & P. Ramirez, 1970. Movimiento Campesino Chileno. ICIRA. Santiago.

Alberti, G., 1970. Los Movimientos Campesinos. In: R. G. Keith et al., El campesino en el Perú. Instituto de Estudios Peruanos. Lima.

Alberti, G., 1972. The breakdown of provincial urban power structure and the rise of peasant movements. Sociologia Ruralis 12, 3/4: 315–333.

Anderson, Ch. W., 1964. Toward a Theory of Latin American Politics. Madison, Land Tenure Centre, Reprint no. 10.

Arroyo, G. & S. Gomez, 1969. Una etapa conflictiva en la reforma agraria. Mensaje, 183–184, October–November.

Barkin, D. & J. W. Bennett, 1972. Kibbutz and colony. Comparative Studies in Society and History 14, 4: 456–483.

Blau, P. M., 1964. Exchange and power in social life. John Wiley & Sons, Inc. New York.

Blok, A., 1969. Variations in patronage. Sociologische Gids 16, 4: 365–378.

Blok, A., 1971. On brigandage with special reference to peasant mobilization. Soc. Gids 18, 2: 208–216.

Boissevain, J., 1966. Patronage in Sicily. Man 1, 1: 18–33.

Bonilla, F. en J. A. Silva Michelena (eds.), 1967. A strategy for research on social policy. M.I.T. Press. Cambridge.

Bourricaud, F., 1967. Pouvoir et Société dans le Pérou Contemporain. Paris, Colin.

Callado, A., 1964. Tempo de Arraes. José Alvaro Ed., Rio de Janeiro.

Cepal, 1967. Evolución y situación actual y futura de la agricultura latino-americana. Santiago, ICIRA. Resumen del documento Cepal E/CN. 12/767/Add. 3/1967.

Cepal, 1969. El pensamiento de la Cepal. Editorial Universitaria S.A. Santiago.

Chodak, S., 1972. From brotherhood to otherhood. Some aspects of social change in modernizing rural Africa. Sociologia Ruralis 12, 3/4: 302–314.

Chonchol, Jacques, 1970. Poder y Reforma Agraria en la experiencia chilena. Cuadernos de la Realidad Nacional No. 4, juni 1970, p. 50–87.

Coser, L. A., 1956. The functions of social conflict. Routledge & Kegan Paul. London.

Cotler, J., 1969. Pautas de cambio en la sociedad rural. In: José Matos Mar et al.: Dominación y cambios en el Peru Rural. Instituto de Estudios Peruanos. Lima.

Cotler, J., 1970. La mecanica de le dominación interna y del cambio social en el Peru. In: J. Matos Mar et alii. El Perú actual. Instituto de Investigaciones Sociales. Mexico.

Cotler, J. & F. Portocarrero, 1970. Organizaciones Campesinas en el Peru. In: J. Matos Mar et al.: El Perú actual. Instituto de Investigaciones Sociales. Mexico.

Craig Jr., W. W., 1969. Peru: The peasant movement of la Convención. In: H. Landsberger (ed.), 1969.

Dandler, J., 1969. El Sindicalismo campesino en Bolivia. Instituto Indigenista Interamericano. Mexico.

Diaz, M. A., 1970. Ayacucho y las communidades del hambre. America Indigena XXX, 2: 307–321.

Doorn, J. A. A. van, 1968. Met man en macht. Hedendaags collectief militantisme. Universitaire Pers. Rotterdam.

Dore, R., 1971. Modern cooperatives in traditional communities. In P. Worsley (ed.) 1971.

127

Elias, N., 1969. Über den Prozess der Zivilisation. Francke Verlag. Bern and München.

Erasmus, Ch. J., 1968. Community development and the Encogido Syndrome. Human Organization 27, 1: 65–74.

Etzioni, A., 1968. The Active Society. The Free Press. New York.

Etzioni, A., 1969. Dual leadership in complex organizations. In C. A. Gibb (ed.), Leadership. Penguin Books. Harmondsworth.

Evers, B. en R. Vossenaar, 1971. Invoervervangende industrialisatie en sectorale prijsveranderingen in Latijns-Amerika. Economie 35, 4: 185–200 and 35, 5: 237–262.

Fals Borda, O., 1968. Las revoluciones inconclusas en America Latina. Mexico, Siglo XXI.

Fals Borda, O., 1970. Formación y deformación de la politica cooperativa en America Latina. Boletin del Instituto de Estudios Sociales y Laborales, abril.

FAO, 1969. Provisional Indicative World Plan, 2 vols. Rome.

Fingarette, H., 1967. On responsibility. Basic books. New York.

Foster, G. M., 1962. The dyadic contract in Tzintzuntzan, II: patron–client relationship. Am. Anthropologist 65, 6: 1280–1294.

Foster, G. M., 1965. Peasant society and the image of limited good. Am. Anthr. 67, 2: 293–315.

Frank, A. G., 1967. Capitalism and Underdevelopment in Latin America. Monthly Review Press. New York.

Friedrichs, R. W., 1960. Alter versus ego: an exploratory assessment of altruism. ASR 25, 3: 498–508.

Galjart, B. F., 1968. Itaguaí – Old habits and new practices in a Brazilian land settlement. Pudoc. Wageningen.

Galjart, B. F., 1969. Patronage als integratiemechanisme in Latijns-Amerika. Soc. Gids, 16, 6: 402–411.

Galjart, B. F., 1971a. Agricultural Development and Sociological Concepts: A critique. Rural Sociology, 36, 1: 31–42.

Galjart, B. F., 1971b. De mobilisatie van boeren in Latijns Amerika. Sociologische Gids, 18, 2: 181–194.

Galjart, B. F., 1974. Allende y los campesinos: un analisis ecologico de las elecciones presidenciales de 1970 en Chile. Boletin de Estudios latino americanos y del Caribe, 16: 50–67.

Glaser, B. G. en A. L. Strauss, 1967. The discovery of grounded theory. Aldine Publishing Company. Chicago.

Gilhodes, P., 1970. Agrarian Struggles in Columbia. In: Stavenhagen (ed.) 1970.

Gomez, S., 1969. Los empresarios agricolas y la reforma agraria. Univ. Catolica de Chile, Escuela de Sociologia. Santiago. (stencil).

Gouldner, A., 1960. The norm of reprocity: a preliminary statement. A.S.R. 25, 2: 161–178.

Hagstrom, W. O. en H. C. Selvin, 1965. Two dimensions of cohesiveness in small groups. Sociometry 28, 30–43.

Hobsbawm, E. J., 1971. Class consciousness in history. In: Istvan Meszaros (ed). Aspects of history and class consciousness. Routledge & Kegan Paul. London.

Horne, A., 1971. Comandante Pepe. Encounter, July.

Huizer, G., 1970. Peasant Unrest in Latin America. Amsterdam (thesis).

Hutchinson, B., 1966. The patron-dependent relationship in Brazil: a preliminary examination. Sociologia Ruralis 6, 1: 3–30.

ILO, 1971. The World Employment Programme. Geneva.

Jolly, A. L. et al., 1970. Estudio economico de los asentamientos ICIRA. Santiago.

Kadt, E. de, 1970. Catholic radicals in Brazil. University Press. London, Oxford.

Kaufman, R. R., 1972. The politics of land reform in Chile 1950–1970. Harvard University Press. Cambridge.

Klatzmann, J., 1972. Les cooperatives de production et le problème de la taille optimale de l'entreprise agricole. Paper presented at 3rd World Congress of Rural Sociology, Baton Rouge.

Laclau, E., 1971. Imperialism in Latin America. New Left Review, 67: 19–38.

Lamond Tullis, F., 1970. Lord and peasant in Peru. A paradigm of political and social change. Harvard University Press. Cambridge.

Landsberger, H., 1967. The labor elite: is it revolutionary? In: S. M. Lipset en A. Solari (eds.): Elites in Latin America. Oxford University Press. New York.

Landsberger, H., 1968. Chile: A vineyard Workers Strike: A case study of the Relationship between Church, Intellectuals and Peasants. In: H. Landsberger (ed.) 1969.

Landsberger, H. (ed), 1969. Latin American Peasant Movements. Cornell University Press. Ithaca and London.

Lehmann, D., 1969. Hacia un analisis de la conciencia de los campesinos. Cuadernos de la realidad nacional, no. 2.

Lehmann, D., 1970a. Bases estructurales y culturales para la capacitación cooperativa. El caso de Putaendo. ICIRA. Santiago. (stencil).

Lehmann, D., 1970b. Puchuncavi: El estado reformista y las estructuras de poder: ICIRA. Santiago. (stencil).

Lehmann, D., 1972. La agricultura chilena y el periodo de transición. ICIRA. Santiago. (stencil).

Mauss, M., 1967. The Gift. Norton & Cy. New York.

McBride, G. M., 1970. Chile: Su tierra y su gente. ICIRA. Santiago.

McClelland, D., 1961. The achieving society. van Nostrand Cy. New York.

McCoy, T., 1969. The politics of Structural Change in Latin America: The Case of Agrarian Reform in Chile. Land Tenure Center, Research Paper No. 37. Madison.

Mintz, S. W. & E. R. Wolf, 1967. An analysis of Ritual Co-Parenthood (Compadrazgo). In: J. M. Potter, M. N. Diaz en G. M. Foster (eds.): Peasant Society. Little, Brown & Cy. Boston.

Mitrany, D., 1961. Marx against the peasant. Collier Books. New York.

Moog, V., 1954. Bandeirantes e Pioneiros, paralelo entre duas culturas. Globo. Rio de Janeiro.

Moraes, Clodomir S. de, 1970. Peasant Leagues in Brazil. In: R. Stavenhagen (ed.), 1970.

Morais, C. Santos, 1969. Algunas consideraciones en torno de las organizaciones campesinas en American Latina. Documento presentado al Seminario sobre la partipación social en America Latina, Mexico.

Mühlmann, W. E. en R. J. Llaryora, 1968. Klientschaft, Klientel und Klientelsystem in einer Sizilianischen Agro–Stadt. J. C. B. Mohr. Tübingen.

Nickel, H. J., 1971. Die Campesinos zwischen Marginalität und Integration. Bertelsmann Universitätsverlag. Düsseldorf.

Olson, M., 1965. The logic of collective action. Harvard University Press. Cambridge.

Pascal, A., 1968. Relaciones de poder en una localidad rural. ICIRA. Santiago.

Paz, Octavio, 1967. El laberinto de la soledad. Fondo de Cultura Economica. Mexico.

Pearse, A., 1970. Agrarian Change trends in Latin America. In: Stavenhagen (ed) 1970.

Petras, J. & M. Zeitlin, 1970. Agrarian Radicalism in Chile. In: Stavenhagen (ed) 1970.

Petras, J. & H. Zemelman Merino, 1972. Peasants in revolt. A Chilean case study 1965–1971. University of Texas Press. Austin and London.

Philipsen, H., 1969. Steekproeven. Universitaire Pers. Leiden.

Powell, J. D., 1969. Venezuela: The Peasant Union Movement. In: H. Landsberger (ed) 1969.

Pugh, R. et al., 1970. Estudios de la realidad campesina: cooperación y cambio. Geneva, United Nations Research Institute for Social Development.

Queiroz, M. I. P. de, 1962. Uma categoria rural esquecida. Revista Brasiliense, January–February: 85–97.

Queiroz, M. I. Pereira de, 1965. O messianismo no Brasil e no mundo. Dominus Editora. São Paulo.

Quijano, A., 1965. El Movimiento Campesino del Peru y sus Lideres. America Latina 8, 4: 43–64.

Quijano, A., 1967. Contemporary Peasant Movements. In: S. M. Lipset en A. Solari (eds.): Elites in Latin America. Oxford University Press. New York.

Ramirez, P., 1968. Cambio en las formas de pago de la mano de obra agricola. ICIRA. Santiago.

Ranitz, C. W. M. de & E. H. de Ranitz, 1972. Resultaten van een vooronderzoek in drie chileense asentamientos. Landbouwhogeschool, Afdeling Niet Westerse Sociologie (Internal report) Wageningen.

Rogers, E. M. & L. Svenning, 1969. Modernization among Peasants. Holt, Rinehart and Winston, Inc. New York.

Röling, N. G., 1970. Adaptions in Development: A Conceptual Guide for the Study of Non-innovative Responses of Peasant Farmers. Economic Development and Cultural Change 19, 1: 72–85.

Salazar, B. A., 1968. La cultura de la dominación. In: Peru Problema. Fransico Moncloa Editores. Lima.

Santis, S. de, 1969. Bewusztsein und Produktion. Eine Kontroverse zwischen Ernesto Che Guevara, Charles Bettelheim und Ernest Mandel über das ökonomische System in Cuba. Kursbuch 18. Suhrkamp. Frankfurt.

Schachter, S., 1961. The psychology of affiliation. Tavistock Publications. London.

Scheidlinger, S., 1958. Freudian concepts of group relations. In: D. Cartwright en A. Zander (eds.). Group Dynamics. Row, Peterson & Cy. Evanston.

Scott, C. D., 1972. Some problems of marketing among small peasant proprietors in Chile. Boletin de Esudios Latinoamericanos, no. 13.

Silva, J. & Chonchol, 1969. El Desarrollo de la Nueva Sociedad en America Latina. 2nd ed. Editorial Universitaria. Santiago.

Simmel, G., 1969. Conflict & The web of group-affiliations, 4th Edition. The Free Press. New York.

Stavenhagen, R., 1966. Social aspects of agrarian structure in Mexico. Social Research 33, 3.

Stavenhagen, R. (ed), 1970. Agrarian Problems and Peasant Movements in Latin America. Doubleday & Company, Inc. Garden City.

Thompson, J. D. & D. R. van Houten, 1970. The behavioral sciences: an interpretation. Addison–Wesley Publishing Company. Reading.

Urzúa, R., 1969. La demanda campesina. Universidad Catolica de Chile. Santiago.

Vilaça, M. V. & R. Cavalcanti de Albuquerque, 1965. Coronel, Coroneis. Edições Tempo Brasileiro. Rio de Janeiro.

Weber, M., 1925. Wirtschaft und Gesellschaft. J. C. B. Mohr. Tübingen.

Weber, M., 1964. Social and economic organization. Translation by A. M. Kenderson & Talcott Parsons. New York, The Free Press. New York.

Weerdenburg, L. J. M., 1970. Sociaal–Economische Differentiatie in de Landbouw. Landbouwhogeschool, Afdeling voor Sociale Wetenschappen, (Bulletin no. 35). Wageningen.

Williams, L. K., 1969. Algunos correlatos sico-sociales de sistemas de dominación. In: Matos Mar, J. et al. Dominación y Cambios en el Perú rural. Instituto de Estudios Peruanos. Lima.

Wolf, E. R., 1956. Aspects of Group Relations in a Complex Society, Mexico. Am. Anthropologist 58, 6: 1065–1078.

Wolf, E. & E. C. Hansen, 1966. Caudillo Politics. Comparative Studies in Society and History, IX, 2: 168–179.

Worsley, P. (ed), 1971. Two blades of grass. Rural cooperatives in agricultural modernization. Manchester University Press. Manchester.

Wright, D., 1971. The psychology of moral behaviour. Penguin Books. Harmondsworth.

Young, F., 1970. Reactive subsystems, A.S.R. 35, 2: 297–307.

Zantwijk, R. van, 1965. Lastdragers en Hoofden. Amsterdam. (thesis).

Subject index